THE FUTURE OF PARTNERSHIP

THE FUTURE
OF
PARTNERSHIP

by
Letty M. Russell

THE WESTMINSTER PRESS
Philadelphia

Scripture quotations from the Revised Standard Version of the Bible are copyrighted 1946, 1952, © 1971,
1973 by the Division of Christian Education of the
National Council of the Churches of Christ in the
U.S.A., and are used by permission.

Book Design by Dorothy Alden Smith

First edition

Published by The Westminster Press ®
Philadelphia, Pennsylvania

PRINTED IN THE UNITED STATES OF AMERICA

9 8 7 6 5 4 3 2 1

Library of Congress Cataloging in Publication Data

Russell, Letty M
  The future of partnership.

  Includes bibliographical references.
  1. Christian life—1960–   2. Man (Christian
theology) 3. God. 4. Freedom (Theology)
I. Title.
BV4501.2.R85   261.8′34   78-20805
ISBN 0-664-24240-5

To My Partner Hans

CONTENTS

PROLOGUE   13

INTRODUCTION   17

PART I
PARTNERSHIP WITH GOD

1/ GOD'S ARITHMETIC   25

     DIVINE ECONOMICS   26
         Household Management   26
         God in Action   28

     PARTNERS IN STEWARDSHIP   32
         Creator, Liberator, and Advocate   33
         New Focus of Relationship   34

     CLUES FROM GOD'S ARITHMETIC   36
         Representative Numbers   37
         One Plus One Equals Three   38

2/ GOD'S UTOPIA   44

     IMAGE OF GOD   45
         Story of Creation   46
         Made in God's Image   47

     PARTNERSHIP AND NEW CREATION   49
         Image and Sexual Polarity   49
         Beginning from the Other End   51

CLUES FROM GOD'S UTOPIA   53
   Divine/Human Partnerships   *53*
   Inequality and Koinonia   *58*

3/ GOD'S SELF-PRESENTATION   61

LORD AND SERVANT   62
   God's History with Humanity   *63*
   Jesus Is Lord!   *65*

PARTNERSHIP AND HIERARCHY   67
   Self-Identity and Power   *68*
   Service in Christian Community   *70*

CLUES FROM GOD'S SELF-PRESENTATION   73
   The Context of Service Is Partnership   *73*
   The Context of Partnership Is Service   *75*

PART II
PARTNERSHIP WITH OTHERS

4/ ESCHATOLOGY AND SEXUALITY   81

MEANING OF HUMAN SEXUALITY   82
   New Perspectives on Sexuality   *83*
   Biblical Views of Sexuality   *86*

MARRIAGE AND ALTERNATIVE LIFE-STYLES   88
   Social Challenges to the Nuclear Family   *90*
   Alternative Family Structures   *91*

SEXUALITY AND PARTNERSHIP   95
   Eschatological Perspectives   *95*
   God's Utopia   *99*

5/ ADVENT SHOCK AND THE CHURCH   101

ON THE WAY TO TOMORROW   102
   Maladjustment with the Present   *103*
   Biblical Images of Christian Community   *106*

FREEDOM IN WITNESSING COMMUNITY   107
   Pluralistic Structures   *108*
   Christian Life-Style   *113*

THE CHURCH AND PARTNERSHIP 115
Eschatological Perspectives *116*
God's Self-Presentation *118*

6/ FLIGHT FROM MINISTRY 121

CALL TO SERVICE IN A NEW AGE 122
God's Call to Freedom *123*
Vocation in the Light of Tradition *123*

CLERGY AND LAITY 126
Oppressors and Oppressed *126*
Changing Roles in Ministry *129*

MINISTRY AND PARTNERSHIP 132
Eschatological Perspectives *134*
God's Arithmetic *136*

7/ LOVING THE QUESTIONS 140

PARTNERSHIP IN LEARNING 141
Participation in God's Actions *143*
Liberation in Community *145*

LIVING THE QUESTIONS 147
Prefigurative Partnership *147*
Acting Our Way Into Thinking *149*

LEARNING AND FUTURE 152
Eschatological Perspectives *152*
God's Partnership *155*

PART III
BEGINNING FROM THE OTHER END

8/ PARTNERSHIP AND THE FUTURE 159

A REVOLUTION IN WHICH EVERYONE WINS 160
Changing Social Structures *160*
Revolution of Consciousness *162*

FUTURE AND PARTNERSHIP 164
Meaning of Partnership *164*
Theology and Changing Consciousness *165*

THEOLOGICAL PERSPECTIVES ON THE FUTURE   167
Thinking About the Future   *168*
Biblical Interpretation   *171*

NOTES   177

GLOSSARY   197

PROLOGUE

The roots of this book extend back to the beginning of my life story and beyond, to the stories of many others who have joined me as partners over the years. I have learned about partnership in the same way as others: by living and experiencing deep pain, ecstatic joy, and steady plodding. I have found only a few clues about why the gift of partnership sometimes withers and other times grows like a mustard seed. I have chosen to write about "The Future of Partnership," not because I know more or even as much as others about this relationship, but because I need to look at my own life to see what it is that God is nurturing in me and others, and because I have found that there are many others who share this need to explore, question, and reflect with me. The book is written so that we can join together as partners in learning.

The occasion for beginning such a book occurred in 1974 when I attended a Consultation of the World Council of Churches on Sexism in the 1970's in West Berlin. The report that led to the most vigorous debate was the one in which women from all parts of the world tried to describe the meaning of partnership. Out of these deliberations came a recommendation for a world study of "The Community of Women and Men in the Church."[1] The next summer I was invited to give a speech that was to be the core of this book at a meeting in Louvain of Pro Mundi Vita and the Lutheran World Federation on Partnership of Women and Men.[2] I continued to work with the World Council of Churches developing the new study and with others on related materials, but it was two years before I reached a place in my own life where writing a book on partnership

13

became a possibility for me. I am grateful for the time to begin writing afforded me by an invitation of the Pacific School of Religion to teach in the summer of 1977 and for the questions and commitment of the students and faculty there and at Yale Divinity School who joined me in these explorations.

For those who are familiar with my writing it will be clear that this Prologue picks up where the final Prologue of *Human Liberation in a Feminist Perspective—A Theology* leaves off. I am following my own advice in trying to find out what it would be like "if they gave a revolution and everybody won."[3] Assuming the background of that book's concern for human liberation, this book explores one of the areas into which liberation might lead us. The style again attempts to be nonsexist in references to women and men and to God, continuing my concerns articulated in *The Liberating Word: A Guide to Nonsexist Interpretation of the Bible.*[4] When I have changed the generic use of masculine language in a quotation, I have enclosed the substituted words in brackets. A consistent focus on the meaning of our participation in God's actions as partners with God in the service of others finds echoes from my pastoral work in East Harlem discussed in *Christian Education in Mission.*[5]

While giving a lecture in Dayton, Ohio, soon after my husband died in 1975, I was asked by a woman, "What is the passion of your life?"[6] I responded in the light of my own loss and said, "To affirm life over death, hope over despair." THE FUTURE OF PARTNERSHIP is written out of that passion, for my life, like that of others, is full of struggles to bring partnership to life and to accept the loss of those who have ceased to be, looking for faith to "give thanks in all circumstances" (I Thess. 5:16–18).[7] The book is dedicated to the one who was and continues to be my partner, the late Hans Hoekendijk. We used to joke that I would dedicate my next book to my spouse, thanking him for all those spouselike services of encouragement, tender loving care, spelling corrections, and so forth. But, instead, I must thank him for his partnership in the writing of this book. Indeed, he is a coauthor, for his ideas have long since become multiplied with my own and his love is part of the fabric of my being.

It is difficult to write about partners who are absent, especially when their presence is actually shaping what you say and do.

Yet each of us experiences the presence of absent ones as well as those who share our joys and sorrows at this moment. In our journey of faithfulness with God and others, we find not one partner but many partners. None of us is single. We are partners with a host of family, friends, and acquaintances at work, down the street, and around the globe. It is only with these cotravelers on the road to tomorrow, and not alone, that we will be able to join God in creating life in the midst of a despairing world.

Many persons have already joined me as partners in the work of this book. They have read, discussed, questioned, and shared in shaping its final form. Some were laypersons and others clergy. They were from many different types of jobs and had many interests. Each person had her or his own journey out of which to discuss partnership. As one person said: "Partnership is highly personal. Talking about it reveals something about yourself and your own partnerships."[8] The book itself reflects something of my own experience as a Christian woman who is white, middle-class, living and working in the United States. Therefore, it is limited to discussion of only a few possible perspectives on partnership with others. Yet, within these limits of context, I have tried to point to the universal dimensions of human experience and the shared commitment of those who follow Jesus Christ. Each reader is invited to find the places where the book does make sense and then to join in the exploration of partnership.

One theme of the book is that we can begin to explore the meaning of partnership from the other end. We can begin from the point of view of New Creation and of what God intends us to become in Jesus Christ. Readers are also invited to do their own theology "from the other end." Thus, for a systematic statement of the theology of partnership on which this book is based, you could read first the final chapter, "Partnership and the Future." Your journey, moreover, may lead you to begin with questions about education in Chapter 7 or with concerns about human sexuality in Chapter 4. Although the chapters of the book are designed to build on one another, it is helpful to read sequentially only if you approach with the question, Does this theology of partnership make sense? Others might well begin in the second part if their primary question is, Does the description of partnership make sense of my experience? For those who have difficulty with some of the more technical language, there is a brief Glossary after the last chapter.

Partnership for Christians is described in this book as *a new focus of relationship in a common history of Jesus Christ that sets persons free for others.* In Part I, "Partnership with God," clues about partnership are derived from the discussion of the freedom of God for us and from us. God's freedom for us is seen in God's willingness to serve us and to invite us to become partners with Christ in service. The clues we learn from God reaching out to us are: Quality, not quantity, is a key element in service; service and not sexuality is the most important key to God's intended purpose for humanity; and service of God is not a form of subordination but of empowerment. In God's freedom from us we discover that God's reality is not necessarily ours and the arithmetic of New Creation is often different. For this reason the arithmetic of partnership is not what we expect: the whole is greater than the sum of the parts; the gifts of the Spirit are not equally distributed; and calculated inefficiency is often the way partnership grows through grace.

Part II, "Partnership with Others," tests out these clues in a variety of areas of human experience of partnership such as life-styles, church community life, ministry, and education. The book then invites each reader to share her or his own questions about partnership so that we may once again give thanks for the human community in which God has placed us as stewards of New Creation.

Part III, "Beginning from the Other End," provides a fuller statement of the theology of partnership on which the whole book is based and concludes with an affirmation of hope as a key to the understanding of partnership.

INTRODUCTION

People respond in a variety of ways when asked to describe partnership. Their responses are reflected out of the contexts of their own life experience, language, and culture. Some look within, trying to find who they are and how to make partners of those various selves searching for a center. Others speak of interpersonal relationships in friendship, marriage, communal living, teams, and recreational activities. Or there are those who first think of larger societal institutions such as church, business, and professional groups. Others focus globally on nations, denominations, economic and political groups, while still others look toward God as partner with God's self and with all humanity. Already we see that the word can extend to almost any human relationship and metaphorically to God as well (Rom. 8:15b–17).

We have a share, or part, with one another, or are associated with one another, not only as in the dictionary listing of: business, husband and wife, dance, game; but whenever people aspire to mutual interdependence.[1] The variety increases to "riotous" proportions as we notice that cutting across all these varieties of partnership listed according to size of inclusiveness (from micro-partnerships to macro-partnerships) are the sorts of assigned roles that are not freely chosen. Such are the relationships of equality and inequality because of "life's unconditionals," such as race, sex, class, health, age. These often set people up in false categories that make them unwilling "partners" in an oppressed group. Those particularly sensitive to this resist the use of the word "partnership." They do not want to use the word because domination and subordination are so often

17

hidden under the mask of an ideology of partnership that is a pretense at equality.

Partnership as a meaningless platitude is to be seen all around us. Women have been unequal partners for centuries. Factory workers who are made partners in industry know that usually the words do not remove exploitation. Calling First World and Third World churches "partners in mission" does not necessarily change the dynamics of financial control. Such partnerships can be clearly exposed for what they are by asking in what sense all parties freely chose to enter or to develop them and what mutual benefits are a continued basis of equality.[2]

Taking into consideration that different qualities are more important than others at different times and in different types of partnerships, we can still identify the basic qualities considered important for partnerships by means of continued reflection and discussion of our own experiences and expectations. They would seem to include at least: (1) *commitment* that involves responsibility, vulnerability, equality, and trust among persons or groups who share a variety of gifts or resources; (2) *common struggle* and work involving risk, continuing growth, and hopefulness in moving toward a goal or purpose transcending the group itself; (3) *contextuality* in interacting with a wider community of persons, social structures, values and beliefs that may provide support, correctives, or negative feedback.[3] There is never complete equality in a dynamic relationship, but a pattern of equal regard and mutual acceptance among partners is essential.

As we move ahead to explore the meaning of partnership as an ongoing relationship, we can begin by using the following working description and then proceed to test it out as we reflect on aspects of partnership with God and others. *Partnership may be described as a new focus of relationship in which there is continuing commitment and common struggle in interaction with a wider community context.* Partnership is always growing and dying, for it is a human interrelationship that is never static. As such we can describe it but never say exactly what a blueprint for partnership would be. Partnership defined in a static image would no longer be able to provide clues to the organic, living, and risky nature of that which we seek not only to describe but also to live.

When such a relationship is alive and growing we usually find the gifts of *synergy, serendipity,* and *sharing.* That is, partners produce an overspill of energy that is greater than the sum of the parts, and that displays unexpected or serendipitous gifts and the impulses to share that energy with others.[4]

What makes a partnership Christian presents us with another set of questions that we will need to reflect on together in this book. Insofar as the words "Christian partnership" seem to convey the idea of blueprint or static standard, they present some difficulties. In addition, the words "Christian partnership," in many persons' minds, convey not only the meaning of one ideal but also the meaning of implied superiority over every other type of partnership.

Perhaps it would be better to speak of *Christians who are partners.* Christians who are partners bring with them into any relationship a central partnership with Jesus Christ. This relationship to Christ does not mean that the Christian is automatically a better partner, because this is not necessarily the case. In fact, in many partnerships the inclusion of Christ may be a *minus* element, because the person is distracted by a divided loyalty to both the other person(s) and the common goal, and to Jesus Christ and the message of God's love. However, the presence of Christ in a partnership can also free the Christian or Christians to be more open to the other(s) because identity in Christ both roots them and opens them toward others as they follow the life-style of Jesus of Nazareth. When a Christian forms a partnership with a non-Christian, Christ is still present as a partner in the relationship because of being a part of that person's self-identity, but the central focus of such a relationship is some other source of common purpose.

In describing partnerships that are intentionally formed in the name of Christ, we could say that they are unique only because of that particular center of focus in Christ, not because of any superiority of the members. *Such a partnership of Christians could be described as a new focus of relationship in a common history of Jesus Christ that sets persons free for others.* This partnership with Christ is described in the New Testament by the word *koinōnia.* The emphasis of *koinōnia,* or community, is on a two-sided relationship of giving and receiving, participation, impartation.[5] It is a form of partnership rooted in the life story of Jesus Christ, yet containing small anticipations of God's intended partnership of New Creation. Thus Paul describes the Lord's Supper with these words about *koinōnia:*

> The cup of blessing which we bless, is it not a *koinōnia* in the blood of Christ? The bread which we break, is it not a *koinōnia* in the body of Christ? Because there is one bread, we who are many are one body, for we all partake of the one bread. (I Cor. 10:16–17)

Coming from the root word *koinos,* "common," *koinōnia* reminds us that Christians in partnership are not extraordinary but are ordinary. Their participation with Christ is not exclusive but is intended as a way of sharing God's love with all people.[6] The root of the word also points us toward the meaning that in Christ we are all one. We share as we do in the communion, yet we do not lose our own identity. We are different members of the same body (I Cor., ch. 12; Gal. 3:28).

PART I

PARTNERSHIP WITH GOD

One way of searching out the meaning of partnership in theological perspective is to begin "from the other end." That is, to look for theological clues about partnership, not in the old story of creation, but in the story of New Creation. In God the New Creation is possible. In fact, this New Creation is constantly breaking into our lives even as we live as part of a struggling and suffering world. Isaiah points the way in reminding us that the Lord says:

Cease dwelling on things gone by, and brooding over past events. Come close and look! Here and now I am doing something new! It already emerges over the horizon. Don't you notice it? I am building a road right through the desert. . . . For I will provide water in the wilderness, and rivers in the barren desert, for my chosen people to drink; the people I have chosen for my service so that they may know and praise me.[1]

The ferment of freedom expressed in the rising consciousness of women and men about issues of partnership is, perhaps, a clue to "something new" and ought to be explored in relation to the New Creation that "emerges over the horizon" and not just in relation to "past events."

Pushing ahead to explore theological aspects of partnership requires us to move out on a pilgrimage, to journey with Abraham and Sarah toward a promise that can be heard, but is not yet seen. In searching for new roles and relationships that might express concretely the possibility of partnership in church and society, we must move *now* to act *as if* we are equally human, equally partners with God in the New Creation, and be

21

ready to pay the cost of our pilgrimage toward God's intended future.

I myself, along with many others, have no question that God created male and female in a relation of equality, complementarity, and community. If there were not some consensus on this, there would be no point in talking about partnership, for persons of both sexes and of various races, classes, and nations have been unequal partners for centuries! But, having granted this, what next? What do we do with our lives, churches, and world where old forms of domination and subordination continue to exist and new forms are barely "emerging over the horizon"?

One place to begin discussing clues for new creation is with God's initiative in becoming a partner with humanity as seen in the Biblical story. The Bible is both Scripture and Script. As *Scripture* it is a record of what God has done and is doing in and through the lives of people and their history. We study the Bible to understand how God acts so that we can participate in those actions on behalf of humanity. Our participation as Christians makes the Bible a *Script* that begins with Jesus Christ and stretches back through the whole story of God's dealing with Israel to creation. It stretches forward into our own life stories and beyond, as we join together with others in the continuing struggle toward a new creation in which God will make all things new!

As Creator, God is free from us and from all creation. God is not just identified with nature which is itself part of creation. Nor is God just identified with our own projections, images, or our particular brand of theology, psychology, or ideology. God is partner whose identity always eludes our understanding. Thus it seems that *partnership with God* is a rather pretentious way of describing our relationship with God. We seem either to have demoted God as one among the many or to have promoted ourselves "a little *higher* than the angels." Yet, if God has chosen to be partner with us in the life, death, and resurrection of Jesus Christ, then surely this unexpected solidarity between Creator and creature should provide a perspective for our search.

As Liberator, God chooses to be free for us and the world in order to liberate us from our own individual and collective sin and oppression. The Biblical story tells us that God chose to be a partner with suffering humanity as Immanuel (Isa. 7:14; Matt. 1:23). In Christ, God came, not to be served, but to serve (Mark 10:45). So we find ourselves drawn into God's love affair with the world, not as orchestrators of God's symphony, but as those invited into a partnership of service and freedom with and for God, with and for others, and for the future.

1

GOD'S ARITHMETIC

The unexpected nature of God's actions in choosing to be with us in a solidarity of suffering humanity is an indication of how partnership with God happens. It happens by God's initiative and in the context of God's New Age. In this Age many things are unexpected: the outpouring of unmerited love, the welcoming of the unwelcome, the strange arithmetic of God's rule. In *God's arithmetic* things don't always add up the same way they do on computer printouts from national or international offices. Instead, we hear that talents which are used multiply, and those saved are lost; that the many sheep are neglected in search of the lost; that workers at the last hour are paid as much as those who worked all day; that the poor are fed and the rich sent empty away. The good news of the New Age is that God's rule is breaking into our lives, and all are invited as partners to understand and live out the arithmetic of that rule.

Partnership itself is a relationship that is characterized by strange multiplication tables. A new focus of relationship in which there is continuing commitment and common struggle in interaction with a wider community context displays characteristics of synergy, serendipity, and sharing. The relationships are not just quantitative, but are qualitative. They produce an overspill of energy greater than the sum of the parts and unexpected gifts that need to be shared. If this is true with human beings, then how much more in a relationship with God? In Jesus Christ, God shares with us in a new focus of relationship that sets us free for others in many unexpected ways.

We can look more closely at the nature of God's arithmetic if we turn to the way God's actions in the world provide an understanding of God's economics. This economy leads then to a discussion of the Trinity as a divine partnership of Creator, Liberator, and Advocate. In the light of this discussion we will then look at possible clues for our understanding of partnership that stem from God's arithmetic.

DIVINE ECONOMICS

We do not always understand the mystery of God's actions or the arithmetic of God's rule, yet in faith we affirm that God does act so that both nature and history move toward the ultimate goal of New Creation. In this time between cross and Parousia we view humanity and the world in the light of hope in God's coming, not just in the future, but now amid the painful realities of this world.[1] As we look at our present history we see the saving action of God present within it not as some separate or special history but as the presence of God's intended future.[2]

The idea of salvation history is not new, for it has roots in the Biblical understanding of history as the medium of God's activity in the redemption of the world and the fulfillment of God's promises. In the New Testament the *eschaton*, or end time, is the time in which history continues so that the gospel may be preached to all nations (Mark 13:10). The gift of the Holy Spirit, another sign of the end stage of history, is for the purpose of fulfillment of the Messianic promises of the evangelization of all the nations (Matt. 24:14).[3] Although the Bible contains many perspectives and themes, it is generally agreed that God's saving and liberating action in history is a central motif that links both the Old and the New Testament. Although we do not find the use of the term "salvation history" in the New Testament, we do find the word *oikonomia* in reference to the divine plan of salvation (Eph. 1:10).[4]

Household Management

The word *oikonomia* is derived from the Greek word for the administration of a household. The word for house is *oikos* and the word for household management or stewardship is *oikonomia*. In I Cor. 4:1 and 9:17, Paul speaks of being entrusted with *oikonomia* (a stewardship, duty) of God as an apostle. Paul views his whole apostolic task as a participation in the divine plan for all creation which "waits with eager longing" for its fulfillment (Rom. 8:18–24). By analogy to *oikos,* Eph. 1:10 refers to God's plan or economy in the management of God's household (the world) as *oikonomia* (a plan for the fullness of time).

The same root word is also used in a connotation very important for ecumenical theology today, for *oikoumenē* refers to the whole inhabited world and to all humankind, and not simply to the unity of the churches. Its connotations are also important for Christian education, because the word *oikodomē* relates the act of building up and edification of the household of God to God's planning and building activity (Eph. 4:29; I Cor. 14:4–5).

Oikonomia was recognized as a basic theological concept by such early church fathers as Irenaeus. He understood its meaning in the light of Paul's writings and interpreted *oikonomia* as "the saving action of God in history reaching through the Old Covenant to its fulfillment in the new covenant in the Incarnation and redemptive obedience of Jesus Christ."[5] It is interesting to note in this respect that the word "theology" was not used in a general sense by the church until the fifth century because of its pagan connotations. *Theologia* was restricted to the understanding of God in Godself (immanent Trinity), while *oikonomia* was used for the work of God on behalf of humanity in the plan of salvation (economic Trinity).[6] The work of theology was called *oikonomia* because this was properly a reflection on God's self-revelation in Jesus Christ and in God's continuing work in the world.

Today there is renewed interest in the use of this word in theology because of its importance for understanding both the Biblical witness and history.[7] *Divine economics* or *oikonomia* refers to the way God works in the world to bring it toward fulfillment in New Creation. It is the focus of concern for many who see so much suffering and destruction in contemporary history. From the point of view of New Creation an eschatological perspective raises the question of evil as a question of stewardship in renewal of the world, and the question of identity as a question of partnership among humanity and with God.[8] The reminder that God is the steward or household manager of all creation and has called us to responsible participation in stewardship of creation is at least a starting point in the struggle to liberate nature, nations, and persons from the destruction brought about by false economics of systemic oppression in the name of profit or power. The reminder of God's action in becoming partner with all humanity points us toward the continuing struggle to express the worth and dignity of all persons.

God in Action

Although theologians such as Karl Barth and Karl Rahner have emphasized the importance of the Trinity in dogmatic theology, most people have long since stopped thinking about the Trinity.[9] Even though they may recite trinitarian formulas in worship with great frequency, Christians do not seem to have any pressing interest in how God can be known in three ways. The word "person" in today's usage indicates a separate, rational being and makes the traditional formula of "God in three persons" sound like three Gods. It is no longer understood in its indication of one divine reality with three significant distinctions or ways of self-revelation.

Perhaps a more direct way to approach the subject of the Trinity is to view it against the background of divine economics and to speak of *God in action*. It is God's sending and saving activity through Jesus Christ and the Spirit that we discover in the Biblical story and in our own lives. It is from this angle of vision that Barth discusses the Trinity at the beginning of his *Church Dogmatics* as the basis for understanding revelation in Jesus Christ, and Rahner urges approaching the Trinity from the perspective of God's self-communication in the economic Trinity.[10] Recently Jürgen Moltmann has also taken this approach in *The Crucified God*. In discussing how God is to be understood in the event of the cross of Christ, he emphasizes that we cannot say who God is in Godself but only who God is for us "in the history of Christ which reaches us in our history."[11]

God-in-action more clearly points us in the direction of a dynamic description of God's purpose and plan for the world rather than a static description of a doctrinal formulation. At the same time, relating the action of God in history to the Trinity provides a basis in tradition for the discussion of the meaning of God's intended liberation of creation. This is important to those doing theological reflection from the perspective of oppression, searching out the meaning of God's liberating action for their lives.[12]

For many women there is a third reason for speaking of the Trinity as God-in-action. The doctrinal formulations are such that the Father-Son metaphor for God has become part of the doctrine itself, leading Christians, sometimes, to assume that the Godhead is male. Women and men who are feminists because they advocate full equality of all persons are looking for other descriptions of God that include both masculine and feminine metaphors, and also ones that move beyond gender.[13] Before turning to look at some of the alternative metaphors, we need to look more closely at the classical formulations of the Trinity and how these might illuminate our understanding of stewardship and partnership.

God's *oikonomia* is God's economic action on behalf of the salvation of humanity and the redemption of the world. This action can be described as the *Mission of God* to be with humanity to liberate us. It is the sending activity of God who sends people, prophets, Christ, Spirit, apostles, and us. God in Godself has two missions or sendings: that of truth in Jesus Christ and that of love in the Holy Spirit.[14] God's action can also be described as the dynamic process of *Tradition* (*paradosis,* Rom. 8:31): God handing over Christ, Christ handing over himself, the Holy Spirit handing over Christ.

In classical theology this action of God is discussed under the rubrics of the *economic* and the *immanent* Trinity. The economic Trinity is a description of God's dynamic communication of love to the world. God relates to us in three ways and we speak of the actions of God in three ways even though these actions to the world are indivisible. What one person of the Trinity does they all do. The immanent Trinity is a description of God's dynamic self-communication of love between the persons of the Trinity. Each divine person, or distinction in being, is coeternal and coequal and fully in the other. This sharing in one another nevertheless does not prevent each from having a distinct character in relation to the other. The distinction has been spelled out in various ways traditionally. It is usually indicated by the relationship of Father, Son, and Holy Spirit. Sometimes the distinction is made by an analogy to human consciousness such as that made by St. Augustine to: being, knowing, willing; mind, self-knowledge, self-love; memory, understanding, will.[15] Whether we speak of the Trinity of economic salvation or of the immanent Trinity, or of other metaphors for understanding God, all such knowledge is an attempt to describe God's threefold way of being partner in God's self and being partner with us.

The Bible is a story of God's love affair with the world, as reflected in the life of Israel and of the church. Therefore it does not contain doctrinal formulations like the classical discussions of the Trinity. Yet the presence of God in and through the incarnate Word "as self-expression of truth and as free directive power in history," according to Rahner, points to the experience of God-in-action and thus to a trinitarian expression of that action.[16] According to Moltmann, the cross itself is the central witness to the Trinity, for here the "Father allows the Son to sacrifice himself in the Spirit."[17]

There are many metaphors to describe God's *oikonomia* or saving action, yet some of these metaphors no longer convey to us the full equality of partnership that they once did. The most basic metaphor used in classical theology to describe the relation of members of the Trinity is that of Father, Son, and Holy Spirit. The relation of the Father and the Son is used by analogy and implies a correspondence of relationships. The experience of human fatherhood and sonship helps to understand the relationship of Jesus to his Divine Father, and the relationship of the Divine Word and the Creator.[18]

Although the predominant word for God in the Old and New Testaments is *theos,* the word for Father *(patēr)* occurs frequently in the New Testament.[19] The word "Father" is used in three ways in the New Testament. As *abba, Father,* the words are used in prayer by Jesus and the church to a God who is responsive and forgiving to "prodigal children" (Mark 14:36; Gal. 4:6; Rom. 8:15–16). *My Father* is used by Jesus to describe the unique relation of the Son to the Father; one of total obedience and commitment to the Father in the work of salvation (Matt. 16:17). *Your Father* is used in instructions on true discipleship. Jesus is the one who reveals the Father so that his followers may become true disciples and children of God (John 1:18).[20]

It is clear from its usage that the trinitarian formula based on the relationship of Jesus to God and on the experience of the gift of the Holy Spirit as a continual witness to the resurrection and power of action in the mission of the New Age cannot be ignored in any careful analysis of the Trinity. Yet it is also clear that what was once a natural expression of the analogy of human relationship is no longer so self-evident to many people living in a different social environment. Emphasis on Fatherhood has served to reinforce patriarchy in Western culture and conveys with it a sense of male dominance and hierarchy which leads people to suggest that the appropriate translation of "abba, Father" in the Lord's Prayer might better be that of "Parent."[21]

Shifting the images to feminine instead of masculine does not do anything to the proportional relationships. God can be as easily spoken of in Mother/Daughter concepts. The parable of the "Prodigal Daughter" conveys the story of God's reconciling love as easily as the "Prodigal Son" (Luke 15:11–32). In fact, the exclusive masculine metaphor no longer speaks as powerfully in a world which knows that a father is not alone the begetter of children, or necessarily powerful, just, and loving. Feminine imagery for God is present in the Bible where God has the compassion of a mother, gives birth, and shelters the people (Deut. 32:11, 18; Matt. 23:37; Ps. 51:1; 131:2; Prov. 1:20–33; 3:19ff.). It is also in church tradition where mystics such as St. Theresa speak of Christ as Mother and some Eastern Churches refer to the Holy Spirit in feminine images or terms.[22]

Because of this, Margaret Farley has suggested that we look at the possibility of using masculine/feminine images of God rather than that of parent/child. She suggests the spousal imagery of husband/wife as a possible metaphor.

> Is it not possible on this account to describe the First Person as masculine and the Second Person as feminine and the bond which is the infinite communion between them (the Spirit of both) as necessarily both masculine and feminine?[23]

This might provide us with a less hierarchical model of partnership that would aid in transforming the "child/parent" relationships that often exist between man and woman in marriages today. Here we would have a trinitarian image of reciprocity, joint sharing in the work of salvation and the missions to the world. Yet again the metaphor is limited if it remains one of relation of male and female, for the partnership of God, as well as human partnership, transcends both "filial" and "spousal" images.

It is very difficult to change images that are so deeply rooted in history, culture, and faith even if they no longer seem to function as they once did; but it is important to work out their significance with care to be faithful in representing the Biblical and church tradition, and in representing those who have experienced their own dehumanization as a result of the misuse of these images. Perhaps the most direct way to speak of God in action is not to emphasize trinitarian formulas but to follow Rahner's suggestion and begin with metaphors of God's saving activity in the world. Here we might seek out eschatological metaphors that point to God's action in bringing about New Creation.

PARTNERS IN STEWARDSHIP

It is ironic that in contemporary usage, two of the most important words in New Testament theology have come to have predominantly financial overtones. Certainly we are most familiar with *oikonomia* in its English derivative, "economics," and *koinōnia* is significantly known in "business partnership." Perhaps this is why it is helpful to emphasize the unexpected and unscientific nature of God's arithmetic. For the actions of God that form the basis of the theological understanding of stewardship and partnership are not simply a matter of "facts and figures." The actions of God point to the mystery of the Trinity in which Creator, Word, and Spirit are One. And, it is this mystery which may provide clues to the fundamental meaning of *oikonomia* and *koinōnia*. As Margaret Farley asks:

> Do we not have here, in any case, a model of relationship which is not hierarchical, which is marked by total equality, and which is offered to us in Christian revelation as the model for relationship with Christ and for our relationships in the Church and with one another?[24]

Creator, Liberator, and Advocate

God's actions are united in one economy of salvation which speaks of the dynamic presence of God in our lives as One who is *for us, and not against us.* In the midst of a symphony of groaning, our hope in God's plan for New Creation makes it possible to speak of God as our *Creator* and continuing source of life; as our *Liberator* who sets the captives (us) free; and as our *Advocate* continually present with us as a witness. Speaking in this way not only focuses our attention on God's actions toward us and the world and avoids the use of personal metaphors, it also helps those who have had little hand in the formulation of traditional theology to speak of their hope for a Liberator.[25]

Those who find themselves in situations of political, social, or personal oppression know deep down in spoken and unspoken ways that they are searching for how it would feel to be free. As they refuse to let their humanity be destroyed and struggle toward liberation in whatever their concrete situation of oppression may be, both individuals and groups look to the God of the exodus and of the resurrection. They look for a God who has known suffering and "Godforsakenness" and has conquered the power of evil through suffering love.

For some, the story of Jesus of Nazareth in Luke 4:18–19 really is good news. "You can see! You can walk! You are free! You can be somebody!" For them, God in Jesus Christ is the *Liberator.* Jesus as Liberator is the first sign of God's New Creation in which death and suffering are overcome by love so that we are set free for others even in the midst of our unfreedom and continued existence in Old Creation. This was the experience of many women and men I knew living in East Harlem in New York City. They began to see Christ as Liberator as they found ways to be someone themselves who could serve others in their community. They learned to live out small signs of freedom in the midst of bad housing, addiction, and poverty because in Christ their new life had already begun.

Persons who are oppressed know deep down inside that they must free themselves together with others. They must somehow have the strength to reach out and take the gift of freedom offered them by God and use it in whatever small ways are possible. The presence of God's Spirit provides this strength, not just as a comforter but as an *Advocate* who comes from God and Christ to carry on God's liberating action in their lives and in the lives of others. This need for an advocate who helps us to speak and to "tell it like it is" before others and to God is expressed in the words of Billy Taylor's song, "I Wish I Knew How It Would Feel to Be Free": "I wish you could know what it means to be me. Then you'd see and agree, everyone should be free."[26]

The Advocate speaks to this longing, for the *paraklētos* described in John is a person of high standing who gives personal support to the defendant by intervening with the Judge on his or her behalf (John 14–16).[27] The image is that of a "helper" and not that of a lawyer or a judge. There is someone who puts reputation on the line for us; who cares for us as One for us and not against us.

Those seeking a liberator and an advocate also look for a *Creator* whose very creation includes them as full members of society and gives them human worth. God as Creator has shown a "good opinion of humanity" in sending the Word to dwell among us (Luke 2:14; John 1:14). In this sense of being "pro-human" God may be said to be a "humanist." As a humanist, the Creator continues to bring life to the world and humanity and invites us to share in the re-creation of human wholeness. The Creator's actions are experienced as those which reach out to us and invite us to find ways of participating in New Creation by caring for the world and for society. Diane Jagdeo, a Sister from the West Indies, expressed this very well in the following way:

> To believe in God . . . is in fact to make a statement about the meaning and dimension of all human existence. . . . I believe that human life is precious and dignified . . . cared for . . . and has a destiny . . . and [that we are] not to give up working for this human dimension.[28]

New Focus of Relationship

We ourselves are involved in God's economics. We are commissioned to share in the work of the economic Trinity (I Cor. 9:17): the work of caring for creation, setting the captives free, and standing as witnesses for and with those who need an advo-

cate. As stewards we are invited to join in God's Action or
Mission in the world. Our *oikonomia* (stewardship) is closely
linked to *koinōnia* (partnership), for it is a new focus of relationship in Jesus Christ that commissions us to participate in God's
Mission of creating a more truly human society of justice, liberation, and hope.

We find what it means to be partners in stewardship by looking at the way God works. We discover that stewards are those
who are *humanists,* sharing in contradicting the present realities
of suffering, want, hunger, and injustice so that human life may
be re-created. Such actions become pro-human when they enable people to participate in sharing their own future together
with others, and to live as subjects of worth and not objects of
manipulation. To be a steward is also to admit one's own need
to be set free from personal and social sin which separates us
from ourselves, others, and God and to receive God's gracious
gift of *freedom.* This freedom is seen in that Christ has called
us to be "friends" and not "servants"; to share as stewards of
God's work of liberation and salvation in and through the personal and social structures in which God has called us (John
15:12–17; I Cor. 7:17).

Lastly, our stewardship includes *advocacy;* using our personal, economic, or social power on behalf of justice and love
for others and standing as "helper" for those who need help
before other people or before God. In our lives all these acts of
stewardship work together as one, even as they do in God's
economy, and they bear fruit, not out of our own puny efforts,
but because they take part with Christ as signs of the firstfruits
of God's New Creation.

The partnership of God in the persons of the Trinity also
provides an image of mutuality, reciprocity, and a totally shared
life. The characteristics of partnership, or *koinōnia,* may be
discovered in their perfection in the Trinity, where there is a
focus of relationship in mutual love between the persons and
toward creation. There is a continuing commitment as a unity
of will and purpose toward the goal of New Creation, and a
common action together on behalf of all humanity. The sharing
together of the persons of the Trinity is so deep and profound
that this mystery is only hinted at by the unexpected overspill
of the promises of God as the history of salvation points beyond

itself to God's continuing partnership in Godself and with humanity.

Thus *koinōnia* in God is also *koinōnia* between ourselves and God and between ourselves and others. In Jesus Christ, God shares with us in a new focus of relationship that sets us free to commit ourselves to work together as stewards of New Creation. Our partnerships take on an unexpected quality because the focus in Christ makes us partners and friends with God. Because of the assurance that nothing can separate us from God, we can risk much in our human partnerships in order to gain the depth of commitment needed for serving a God who has chosen to serve humankind.

CLUES FROM GOD'S ARITHMETIC

God's arithmetic is basically eschatological. It begins "from the other end" and often does not appear "to add up right" in the perspective of the present world. Yet it is that eschatological arithmetic which makes it possible to search out clues to the meaning of God's intended partnership in New Creation. Thus Paul tells us:

> When anyone is united to Christ, there is a new world; the old order has gone, and a new order has already begun. (II Cor. 5:17, NEB)[29]

We should not be surprised at the unexpected quality of the way God counts and measures, for what little the Bible reveals to us of the mystery of God's action indicates that the "new order" means "new math." In the Biblical accounts the liberating dynamic of God's action often stands out as a paradox in the midst of the expectations and social situations of the old order. More often than not, glimpses of the new order are revealed through suffering and defeat, at points of weakness and despair, not just at moments of victory and joy. God speaks out of captivity and cross, and not just out of exodus and resurrection. Even God's actions in themselves appear contradictory. Some clues of this eschatological arithmetic are that it often turns out to be either much *less* than we expect or far *more* than we dared hope.

Representative Numbers

Hans-Ruedi Weber, in his article entitled "God's Arithmetic," has pointed out that in both the Old and the New Testament

> it is not the many who become agents of God's mission of reconciliation for all, but the few who are so weak that they must put all confidence in God's strength.[30]

Redemption of the whole world comes through the history of a tiny nation and then through the One Member of that nation chosen to give his life as a ransom for all (Mark 10:45).

In God's eschatological arithmetic the increase in numbers is seen as a qualitative sign of the New Age, not as a quantitative validation of God's *oikonomia,* or of the plans of human beings who consider themselves to be "God's ground personnel." According to Weber, mission is much more directly connected with sacrifice than statistics. "Numbers and growth are important in God's arithmetic: not necessarily large and increasing numbers, but representative numbers and growth in grace."[31] Growth in grace and faithfulness often leads to a numerical decrease in church membership.

Partnership in God's stewardship of New Creation involves us in representative numbers whether they turn out to be ones that increase or decrease. As stewards we are called to be a representative part of the whole; to be communities of Christians who are like salt or leaven in the world (Matt. 5:13; 13:33). This is hard for us to accept, no matter what our circumstances. For, if we are part of a growing and wealthy congregation, we would rather not hear that the "kingdom of heaven" may be represented by the few, the poor, the marginal. And, if we are part of the few, the poor, the marginal, we would rather be among the numerous, rich, and powerful. Yet partnership in God's *oikonomia* means living and working in a situation "as if not"; looking for ways to represent the coming future by signs of cooperation on behalf of others. Thus Paul says of his own ministry:

> I have learned to find resources in myself whatever my circumstances. I know what it is to be brought low, and I know what it is to have plenty. I have been very thoroughly initiated into the human lot with all its ups and downs—fullness and hunger, plenty

and want. I have strength for anything through him who gives me power. (Phil. 4:11–13, NEB)

Even one person can make a difference when his or her stewardship is looked at from the perspective of partnership in New Creation. A person who is a "token" in an organization is not necessarily alone or powerless. A Christian woman or black, for example, in such a situation continues to be partner in God's *oikonomia* and with other women or blacks. Looking at the situation as a possible setting for God's humanizing change can empower the person who ceases to be "just a token" regardless of arithmetic. The position can be used as a pressure point to include other marginal people, especially if the person works with others who form a network of information. It also becomes a representative position when it is genuinely exercised in partnership with God, and with others who form a support and accountability group for the person serving in the token position. The person may not yet be a partner in the organization, but she or he can be a partner with others who share a common concern, to eliminate subordination because of sex or race.

In the same way very small groups of Christians can often help to make a difference when the partners in the group see themselves as representative numbers. This happened in a small group of church-employed women in New York City. They became concerned about the participation of women in the Fifth Assembly of the World Council of Churches meeting in Nairobi in December 1975. There were only a dozen or so, but they began to talk with others and to develop a U.S. Working Group on the Participation of Women in the WCC which could cooperate with the staff and churches of the WCC in helping to see that the recommended 20 percent women delegates were at the Assembly and that there was support for continuing cooperation among women and men in the World Council.[32] The original small group was not alone. It saw itself as part of a representative number and acted on behalf of the whole in order to support fuller unity in the church.

One Plus One Equals Three

God's strange arithmetic means that, although representative numbers can lead to lack of "worldly success," there is also a marvelous *multiplication table* in the way God works in the *oikoumenē*. God sometimes adds to the number of those who are being saved (Acts 2:47). When there is a new focus of relationship in Jesus Christ, the One Partner becomes 12, becomes 500, becomes 5,000, and so on! In ordinary math, one plus one equals two, or one times one equals one, but in the New Creation there is often an overspill, so that one plus one becomes three or more.

This multiplication is activated in our lives through the work of God's Spirit, as the Advocate continues to bear witness to the power and presence of Christ in the world. It can be seen in the metaphor of the partnership of God in the Trinity. Here one plus one equals three because the Son is "begotten" of the Father, and the Spirit "proceeds from the Father and the Son" according to Western tradition. This act of "spiration" is God's communication of love to the world that continues so that we are drawn into the sending action of God. All who respond to this invitation of God's love find that even partnerships of two become three because of the presence of God's Spirit. These partnerships in turn begin to share the Spirit of God so that three becomes more in the sharing of gifts.

The question of arithmetic has been one that has been important to Christian feminists in discussing the partnership of men and women. Looking at the story of Adam and Eve in Gen. 2:24, they question whether it is possible to "become one flesh," if that means that literally two become one. They point out that in the predominant styles of partnership this oneness signifies not just the deep physical and spiritual relationships possible between woman and man, but rather that one (the woman) loses her identity, her name, and sometimes even her property, becoming an appendage of her husband.

Many feminists reject this arithmetic and for good reason. A partnership is only strong where the partners each are whole, growing, and separate persons whose own identity is not lost, but enhanced in the relationship. In this sense the two remain two with separate identities within and outside the partnership relationship. Perhaps the discussion of two becoming one, or two remaining two would be helped by looking at partnership in the New Creation. Here God's arithmetic often, according to the words of Jesus, seems to work otherwise. The model of *koinōnia* begins, not with two, but with One. It begins with Jesus, who does not appear to have been married, yet who managed to evoke in others a solidarity of relationship that produced a multiplication of *koinōnia.*

In the New Creation male and female can have a variety of relationships that are not necessarily biological or cultural. Perhaps a clue to this comes from the words of Jesus in Mark 12:25. He responds to the Sadducees by saying that in the resurrection "they neither marry nor are given in marriage." These words do not say that there is no male or female but that the relationships transcend the existing laws and customs. Developing church traditions took this to mean that celibacy was a preferable state of life in the beginning of the New Age, and some interpreted the passage to mean that everyone in heaven becomes male (overcomes all deficiencies!).[33] Yet Paul reminds us in I Cor. 7:25–31 that in the end times all relationships are "as if not," put under the call of Christ to mission and service. The most important aspect of relationships is whether they multiply gifts in such a way that the Spirit of Christ continues to be shared with others.

Not only does the partnership of God come in threes and not twos, but also the partnership, or *koinōnia,* of Christ comes in two or three gathered in his name (Matt. 18:20). Two seem constantly to become more than two in the sense that wherever *koinōnia* and *oikonomia* are found together, there is often a multiplication into thousands. This helps to remind us that there is no one form of partnership and therefore it is best to inform our analogies and images of partnership out of our understanding of God's *oikonomia* and action in the Trinity toward New Creation rather than by focusing on Genesis and the Old Creation.

Those who have experienced the gift of partnership (men/women; women/women; men/men; mixed groups) in any deep and profound way know that in each such relationship the gifts of the Spirit mean that the whole becomes an overplus of the sum of the parts. This has happened to me in many relationships, such as partnerships in parish churches, in interracial groupings, on task forces, among teachers and students in classrooms, among women across continents. I have certainly experienced it in my own marriage. I became more than myself because of my husband and he became more than himself because of me. Hans was an excellent linguist and I was very poor at languages. He was such a perfectionist that he had difficulty writing for publication, while I was willing to commit myself to print. Together we were able to do a better job of research and writing than either could do alone. His health was so fragile that our gratitude to God for shared life and love was multiplied and channeled into an exciting partnership through teaching. We were at least three or more as we rejoiced in the gifts each brought to the service of Christ in the New Age.

Whether we are Christians or not, God has created us in such a way that the presence of love in a relationship means that it will multiply. Even a simple relationship of two people really involves at least six relationships, for love is toward "me, you, and us." Each person loves self. Each person loves the other, and also loves the collective partnership that is on its way to being shared with others.

One plus one equals three or more because partnerships have a common goal beyond the persons involved and a wider context of relationships with which they interact. Sometimes partnerships grow because of the bearing of children. But the growth of the children and parents is enhanced as they move beyond the small family unit to care for and interact with others. Each must grow as a whole person in his or her own right so that the arithmetic has a plus factor. Such a family would be a "close encounter of a third kind," for it would always have other common goals and outside commitments that would help the encounter stay healthy instead of being closed in on itself.

When one plus one equals one there is not only loss of full selfhood of some of the partners, but also there is devastating pain when a partner is lost. One minus one equals zero. Sometimes when a woman loses her husband through divorce or death she finds herself unable to believe that she can cope at all, because she has been led to find her identity only in him, and not in herself and in her commitment to others and God. Partnerships do dissolve, and the loss always causes pain and insecurity. But lost partnerships can be appreciated and even counted as gift if the two are two or more, so that the loss of one still leaves whole persons to move forward on a new journey.

Partnerships also grow through the shared commitment to action that is the center of the relationship. An example of this purpose of partnership is seen in the Ujamaa way of life in the Tanzanian policy of socialism through extended family units of production. In this policy people are encouraged to live together in Ujamaa villages and to share in ownership of land and means of production as well as in an equal distribution of wealth. In writing about this way of life that has been developed out of the tradition of African familyhood, Bishop Christopher Mwoleka of Rulenge, Tanzania, says:

> I am dedicated to the ideal of Ujamaa because it invites everyone, in a down to earth practical way, to imitate the life of the Trinity which is a life of sharing.[34]

Another group working out a form of partnership through shared action is the Senior Gleaners, founded in 1976 to help deal with the hunger problem. It is composed mainly of low-income retired persons who travel around California picking up fruit and vegetables after harvest. In 1977, the 1,700-member organization gleaned over four hundred tons of produce which they distributed not only among themselves but to thirty charities as well. Homer Fahrner, the seventy-five-year-old founder, saw the Senior Gleaners as a self-help group, but gradually the self-help has grown into a partnership with many other organizations and people.[35]

God's eschatological arithmetic is evident both in the divine economics of God's saving action in history and in the relationship of the partners of the Trinity among themselves. This arithmetic often means unexpected mathematical equations in our own lives and partnerships. As partners in God's *oikonomia* we look for small signs of the New Creation and seek to be faithful even when our role in Christian community is that of a remnant or representative number. At other times our partnerships with God and one another may receive the power of God's love in such a way that they multiply like the seed sown in good soil (Matt. 13:8). In any case a clue to the way we live our lives as stewards of God's intended future is that we should not be surprised at either scarcity or abundance. Rather we can be thankful that God has called us into a divine-human partnership and, sometimes, multiplies the grace of our partnership with others as well.

2

GOD'S UTOPIA

In a society of rapid change, existence itself has become questionable, and we are driven to search for our own identity and meaning. All sorts of answers are shouted at us from the media; gossiped among family and friends; and proclaimed in pulpits and classrooms. But who shall *we* choose to be? Like the demoniac of Mark 5:1–20 we are Legion![1]

Some of us search for our identity in psychological theories and analysis. Others turn to our own history and that of society to find what has gone wrong with our world and ourselves. Still others of us turn to our religious traditions. If we turn to the Bible, asking the question Who am I? we are frequently startled by the point of view we find. For Scripture begins from the other end. It is God who questions and addresses us. God asks Adam, "Where are you?" and Cain, "Where is Abel your brother?" (Gen. 3:9; 4:9). The divine initiative is clear in the stories of Moses, the fugitive from justice: "I will be with you"; Mary, the humble young woman: "Hail, O favored one"; and Jesus, the rabbi, "This is my beloved Son" (Ex. 3:12; Luke 1:28; Mark 9:7). The clue the Bible gives is this: What we are is related to the mystery of God's deciding to be with us. In Jesus Christ, God addresses us and provides a living relationship to help us shape the present and future of our lives.

This partnership with God involves the comforting and disturbing presence of One who tells us who we are. Immanuel ("God with us," Isa. 7:14) is the Biblical answer to our sincere quest for identity. We are those addressed by God to become what God intends us to be: human beings, able to relate in love to ourselves, to others, and to God. We are addressed by God

to become partners. In this sense *we are God's utopia*. We are
created by God and set free to become witnesses to a New
Creation.

Those who say that the search for identity in God's future
made present and anticipated in the Christ event is "utopian"
miss the point. As Moltmann says, "We believe in God because
God believes in us and the world."[2] Our faith leads us to seek
ways to live out our lives as signs of God's promised future.
Insofar as we raise up these small signs, God's utopia is becoming present in the midst of the contradictions of our lives and
world.

The utopia in which we already participate, by God's grace,
is not a spatial reality or "place." It is not an expression of God's
presence either above or outside, or even within us. Rather, it
is a temporal reality, an expression of God's presence both in
history and with us, and yet beyond in history and ahead of us.
According to Hans Küng, God is *"the future reality, the one who
is to come, who bestows hope."*[3] Through hope we are drawn into
that future, becoming God's utopian agents of change.

In discussing what God intends us to become as partners, we
must turn to one of the sources of our "memory of the future":
the story of human creation in God's image. But we must, at the
same time, turn to other sources for our understanding of God's
intention by looking at partnership in the light of New Creation.
God's utopia seen in both Old and New Creation will then
provide some clues for us about our identity as partners.

IMAGE OF GOD

In approaching the question of the meaning of the image of
God from an eschatological point of view, we cannot ignore the
fact that "myths of origin" and "myths of *eschaton*" are interrelated. As the Biblical view of New Creation slowly developed
in the prophetic period and was reshaped with the coming of
Christ, the images used were drawn from the stories of creation
and exodus. The *new* was always in tension with the *old* because
the "new thing" God was doing could not be imaged without
recourse to the history of God's faithfulness in the past. Nevertheless, in the eschatological theology of the New Testament,
New Creation was new not only as compared with sin but also

as compared with creation.[4] Jesus, the Son of Man, was not just a mere repetition of the old Adam, but a new outpouring of grace and the possibility of new life for all humanity (Rom. 5:12–17).[5] Although we look to the beginning to understand the Biblical interpretation of God's intention for creation and for us, we expect more at the end than at the beginning. God's promises throughout history have had a constant factor of surprise. The fulfillment is always different from what was experienced and expected.

Story of Creation

The myths of origin in Genesis 1–11 are an attempt of the Hebrew people to explain the relation of Creator and creation from the point of view of those who had experienced liberation in the exodus and the formation of a national and religious identity. The writers want to explain how this experience of salvation and blessing is also reflected in God's faithfulness and care as Creator from the beginning.

The nature of the image of God is itself a mystery. It has been the subject of deep theological discussion for centuries. Because the text in Genesis 1 chooses to be ambiguous, we are likely to read our own interpretation into it. This interpretation is necessary because the question of our identity and of what God intends us to become is one that must be addressed over and over by theology in the light of questions arising out of contemporary experience. Yet such interpretation should be done with care and checked against other indications of God's intent in the whole story of God's promise on the way to fulfillment.

If we stay literally with the Biblical text, there seem to be two alternatives. First, there is some unspecified *similarity* of male and female and God as indicated in Gen. 1:27. Second, there is the image as *dominion:* human beings as God's vice-stewards or partners in caring for creation as indicated in verse 26. Male and female are fully in the image of God as whole human beings and there does not seem to be the implication that each is a "half person." Nor is there any indication that sexuality is the key to the image. The Yahwist version in chapter 2 seems to indicate that, as Dietrich Bonhoeffer says, "Sexuality is nothing but the ultimate realization of our belonging to one another."[6] But the only indication of sexuality here in the Priestly version is that human beings are created in two sexes and can fulfill God's blessing in "being fruitful" as well as "having dominion" (Gen. 1:28).

In Genesis 1 both woman and man are in the image of God and we can speak of God metaphorically as having both male and female characteristics. The customary English translation of *'ādām* in verse 27 as *man* has no justification, for the word is clearly generic and is more correctly translated as "let us make *humankind* in our image."[7] The misunderstanding of this passage has often led to the assumption that *man* is the image of God and therefore God is masculine.

The second creation account in Genesis 2 does not mention the image of God, yet the implied description of the Creator's intention for man and woman is similar. They are created to be in relationship to each other and God and to be responsible for caring for creation as God's representatives.[8]

The continuation of the Yahwist narrative in the story of the Fall indicates that man and woman continue to be treated equally in terms of responsibility for disobedience and in punishment (Gen. 3). The Hebrew of verse 6 says that Adam was *with her* during the discussion with the serpent, and was not ignorant of the temptation. The result of their disobedience was not death but life as struggle for existence outside the garden. The woman is to be subordinate to her husband and to have pain in childbirth. The man is to be subordinate to the ground out of which he was taken and to have pain in tilling the soil. This description of the existing cultural pattern by the writer is understood as God's decree in fallen creation, but not *"as God's true intention for humankind."*[9]

Made in God's Image

As we have seen, our identity as God's creatures made in God's image is not entirely clear from the exegesis of Genesis 1. All we know is that there is a similarity, and that it has something to do with the work we are given to do in partnership of dominion over creation. That this image has to do with our relationship to God, one another, and the world can, perhaps, be inferred.

If we move to ask what that might mean in theological terms, we might be able to say with Bonhoeffer that there is at least an "analogy of relationship" here, if not an "analogy of being."[10] Just as God is free from and yet for creation, human beings are free from creation, yet they move beyond it in their ability to give it meaning through personal and social history.[11] At the same time, they are free for creation, because God's intention is that they share God's stewardship of bringing creation toward its fulfillment.

This relational aspect of human beings is at the core of their existence, which is shaped by their relation to others and God. It is a fact of our human condition that we are made not only in God's image but also in the image of our culture.[12] The human ability to go beyond ourselves toward others in order to realize our own being may be described as self-transcendence or transeunce. Persons are transeunt when they operate beyond themselves in order to become themselves. "Transeunt" is a form of the word "transient," which signifies "going beyond itself." It comes from the Latin *transire*, "to go beyond."[13] Our ability and desire to go beyond ourselves is expressed both individually and collectively, and in many different and even opposite ways. One person may express transeunce in terms of complete unity and identification with the cultural environment, and another in terms of complete rejection.

The quality of transeunce can also be a description of human beings as historical: always in the process of going beyond the present, and beyond themselves toward the future. This historical characteristic is frequently described by the existentialists in terms of transcendence. Thus Gabriel Marcel describes our need for transcendence in terms of hope as the driving force behind what it is to be human.[14] Because of the historicity of human beings it seems better to speak of transeunce than transcendence, since the emphasis is on the *beyond in history and existence,* and not the beyond, above or outside of history. The relatedness of human persons is always situated in history, and God's relatedness takes place in and through history.

Human transeunce points to the relational image of God. Because we were created to be in relation to God, self, and neighbor, we seek to find ourselves in going beyond ourselves toward others. In Christ we see true self-transcendence or transeunce in his "being for others."[15] Christ finds his identity as the Servant Messiah in giving himself to others and to God. His

saving work has brought about a New Age in which humanity
is placed in relation to God and neighbor and all are invited to
share in the acceptance of this reconciliation. In attempting to
interpret the meaning of our identity as those made in God's
image, we find that we are constantly drawn to interpret the
image not alone out of Genesis but also out of our own understanding of human experience and also out of the New Testament, as we look forward toward anticipations of New Creation.

PARTNERSHIP AND NEW CREATION

A large number of theologians would grant that the understanding of the image of God and of the meaning of true humanity is derivative from the representation of Jesus Christ as the
Second Adam and bearer of new humanity.[16] They nevertheless
usually look to the First Adam and to Eve in the discussions of
the *imago Dei.* These investigations of the creation and fall point
to the *theomorphic* analogy between God and man and woman,
and to the close relationship of mutual love and responsibility
between them. The themes are similar to those discussed above
in relation to Genesis 1–3. Sometimes the investigations include
the meaning of partnership of man and woman, and sometimes
it is relegated to a later discussion of marriage.

Image and Sexual Polarity

In his book on *Man as Male and Female,* Paul K. Jewett
points out that theologians have, broadly speaking, followed
"three schools of thought about sexual polarity" in relation to
the image of God.[17] Either they have maintained the view that
true humanity transcends sexuality and is basically androgynous. Or they have maintained that the male/female distinction
is not an essential part of the doctrine, although both women
and men share in the divine image. Or, lastly, they have held
that the image of God is to be male and female and sexuality
is the bearer of the image of God.[18]

Although I recognize that the creation accounts are of great
importance for any consideration of the meaning of human
identity and relationship, it appears to me that they are an
unfortunate starting point for investigations of partnership. Not
only is the meaning of the image of God ambiguous, but also

the creation accounts of Adam and Eve lead to a very narrow range of images for investigating the possibilities of relationships of women and men in partnership. The clues to be found in Genesis to what it would mean to become what God intends us to be as God's utopia are limited.

Those who are searching for new forms of partnership find, first of all, that they are bound to become engulfed in a continued struggle over hermeneutics in relation to Genesis 1–3, reminiscent of the fundamentalist debate over evolution. There is no one way to interpret the stories of creation. They are not in themselves doctrines, and the clues they give are ambiguous. Secondly, we will find that all the various views mentioned in the Jewett typology present difficulties for Christian feminists who are seeking equality for women and men.

Those exploring androgyny find little evidence that the Genesis stories had this in mind. Many feminists today use the word "androgyny" in a positive sense as an indication of wholeness and mutuality.[19] Yet it is formed out of a dualistic concept of humanity and seems to emphasize relationships between persons as those between two halves rather than whole persons.[20] If the original or ideal human was created androgynous, then male and female as separate persons represent a fall from the ideal and are in need of reunion in order to be whole. Those who follow Jungian psychology emphasize "contrasexuality" *within* each person, so that females have an *animus,* or male contrasexuality, and males have an *anima,* or female contrasexuality. This view emphasizes the integration of the androgynous self and warns against projection of our contrasexuality onto others of the opposite sex, and fear of that part of ourselves. But such views tend to reinforce sexual stereotypes by assigning female characteristics to the *anima* and male characteristics to the *animus.*[21]

Those who describe sexual polarity in relation to the image of God according to Jewett's third school of thought emphasize male and female distinctions as grounded in the image of God. This view is expounded very profoundly by Karl Barth and is helpful in underlining the interrelatedness between human beings and God, and between each other. However, there is little evidence, as we have seen, for asserting that human sexuality is the bearer of the image of God in the text of Genesis 1. In addition we find that Barth's argument from God's ordering of creation moves to the assertion that the male/female distinction means that in the unchangeable order of relationship, man is always *A* and woman is always *B* according to God's command.[22] Such a conclusion may be a basis for complementarity in which each has his or her own place and fit, but it is hardly a basis for mutual partnership in which there is no one place or fit and no roles unchangeably fixed as *A* or *B*.

Those who follow the second route hold that male/female distinctions are not central to the discussion of the image. They then find themselves trapped into considering the meaning of partnership of man and woman separately from what it means to be human, usually discussing it under the rubric of marriage and procreation according to Jewett.[23] However, in my opinion, they can also begin the discussion of both the image and partnership from the eschatological perspective of the New Creation. This is not inconsistent with the Biblical view of history which looks to the liberating and saving action of God as an interpretive perspective. The Genesis prologue itself was written in this perspective, for creation was understood in the light of exodus. Those who begin with Old Creation, forgetting God's promised future, are likely to lose sight of the eschatological dimension of partnership as seen in the *koinōnia*-creating presence of Christ in their lives.

Beginning from the Other End

As we have seen, it is characteristic of both Old and New Testament writers to begin from the other end. Not only do they tell us that our identity comes from God and not the other way around, so that we are God's utopia and not God ours, but also they tell us of an expectation of the *new* in God's promised future. These eschatological views sometimes led to quietism and withdrawal from the world. Yet there is much that can guide us today as we seek out the emerging new person.[24]

Therefore, I would propose that we begin from the other end, exploring the meaning of the new humanity in Jesus Christ as *anthrōpos* (human) and not just *anēr* (male). I would not deny Barth's contention that humanity is always expressed as male and female. However, I would contend that, as important as sexuality is in the lives of each of us, the image of God has more to do with transeunce and service of others, and that this is best expressed in many varieties of partnership. Partnership is itself a key to our understanding of identity. For in partnership with Christ we receive our identity as Christians and learn to express our human sexuality in transeunce for others.

Before continuing the discussion of servanthood and human sexuality in the next two chapters, we need to look more carefully at the New Testament perspective on partnership and at the clues for partnership discovered through our discussion of the identity of human beings as God's utopia.

If we turn to the New Testament to see how the presence of Christ shapes the understanding of identity and partnership in the early church, we discover that the two Greek words most frequently used for partnership are *koinōnia* and *metochē*. The semantic spectrum of these words pushes us way beyond any description of male and female and beyond the type of partnership described in Genesis 1 and 2. *Koinōnia,* the most important word for sharing with someone or something, usually stresses a common bond in Jesus Christ (a participation in and with Christ) that establishes mutual community.[25] *Metochē* is also used to indicate having a share in something. The words are sometimes used interchangeably. Paul uses both in II Cor. 6:14 in warning against marriage to unbelievers, and in I Cor. 10:14-22 his description of participation in the "cup of blessing" and the "bread we break" uses the two synonymously. Hebrews 2:14 uses both words in describing the sharing of flesh and spirit between believers and Christ.

The type of sharing, partnership, participation, or communion that these words describe focuses on our relationship in Jesus Christ and with one another in service. Paul and the early church are expressing the meaning of eschatological existence, not in the light of Genesis, but in the light of the Christological model of the New Adam who realizes God's intent for humanity.[26] There is participation with Christ and the Holy Spirit (Heb. 3:14; 6:4; II Cor. 3:4). And there is participation in the Lord's Table, suffering, and glory (I Cor. 10:14-22; II Cor. 1:7; Heb. 12:8; I Peter 5:1). There is also participation in a heavenly calling, in mission, and in sharing with the poor (Heb. 3:1; Rom. 15:26).

As we saw in Chapter 1, the emphasis of *koinōnia,* or community, is on a two-sided relationship of giving or receiving, participation, impartation, fellowship.[27] It is this word and its variants that are so frequently used in the New Testament to describe what happens when there is a new focus of relationship (a common history of Jesus Christ) that sets us free for others. The New Testament understanding of *koinōnia* gives us a clue to the theological understanding of partnership of women and men and of all sizes and groupings of Christians. A new event of God's traditioning action in Jesus Christ results in a focus of *koinōnia* that sets us free for *diakonia*.

CLUES FROM GOD'S UTOPIA

An understanding of God's utopia as God's intention for the new creation of humanity provides us with clues about how partnership might be part of God's purpose. Such an understanding can only provide *clues* and not a *conclusion,* because we are describing an ongoing process.[28] All our partnerships are unfinished; partaking of the longed-for future, yet not yet fulfilled. And our theological reflections on the questions about partnership arising out of experience lead to clues but not to final principles. We find clues to follow and test with our lives, but not final principles, for we are called to live out the story of Jesus Christ in ever-new circumstances. When a person and not a principle is at the center of our life the relationship itself is never static. This means that the meaning of God's intention for creation and the image of God cannot be described in static terms. Instead of drawing a final conclusion we look for some clues about divine/human partnerships and about the problem of equality between men and women, and between all those who are brought together in partnership relations.

Divine/Human Partnerships

We have talked about the possibility of an analogy of relationship and an interpretation of the image of God as transeunce: the ability to move beyond self toward others and God's future. Yet there always remains a qualitative difference between divine and human partnership. God remains a mystery that is expressed in God's freedom *from* us, and not just in freedom for us. Secondly, as we saw in Chapter 1, it is only in the Trinity itself that there is a complete equality of partnership. The members of the Trinity can be said to be fully partners in a unity of witness, sending, and divine communication of love among Creator, Liberator, and Advocate. Thirdly, the relation of partnership established by God with humanity in freedom for us is a covenant relationship of faithfulness in which God remains steadfast in spite of human failure.

Human partnerships even in their unfinished character do, however, participate in the same relational ability to be self-transcendent and go beyond self toward others. Human partnerships have in themselves an element of mystery. We never know ourselves or others completely, even though we seek to become partner with the totality of ourselves and with others. Our partnerships also remain free *from* as well as *for* others. The members of a partnership must have sufficient overlap in their freedom for one another that they are able to fit, yet they must also remain sufficiently independent and free from one another so that their lives are not collapsed into one another's lives.

Although there is never a complete equality in human partnership, a pattern of equal regard and mutual acceptance of all the partners is essential. This is especially difficult in male/female relationships because as Janet Chafetz has pointed out in her book *Masculine/Feminine or Human?* "genders are anything but equal in this society and most others."[29] Yet truly open and honest communication, mutual respect, and the concomitant emotions of warmth and deep affection can only result when interactions are among equals.

The commitment made in partnership is never one in which we can be sure we will be faithful. All relationships entered into by Christians are lived in the threefold tension of the "already, not yet" of the *eschaton*. We are *already partners* even before we know one another, because God has reached out to us in Jesus Christ and has reconciled us, making us partners of one another and God. But we are also always in the process of *becoming partners.* And this is very difficult. It involves partnerships where commitments are broken, and persons betrayed, as well as the few relationships where there are signs that partnership might be a possibility. And at the same time we live in the hope that *we will become partners,* when the provisional signs of *koinōnia* in this life are realized fully in God's promised future. We are all partners, yet we experience not only growth but decline as we search out ways of living now, as if our relationships were those of full partnership.

There are many ways of looking at the question of how relationships become partnership, and the ways have to be spelled out in relation to different settings, some of which are represented in Part II of this book. Even here, however, there is still a broad spectrum of possibilities for how one concretely enters into this or that partnership. Although one can analyze the social dynamics of partnerships as they exist and the roles played in them, there always remains the question: When is a relationship a partnership?

Certainly partnership cannot be attributed to every primary relationship and never to secondary relationships. Primary relationships refer to interactions where there is usually a degree of emotional commitment present as among friends or family. Secondary relationships refer to ritualized interactions for a limited purpose.[30] Primary relationships may be ones assigned and not freely chosen, and they may be anything but mutual. Secondary relationships, on the other hand, are sometimes the way persons choose to enter larger institutional relationships in church or society where there is a high degree of commitment toward a common goal.

The answer to our question is perhaps to say that there is no one way partnerships happen, nor is there a certain limit on the number, duration, or type of partnerships established by a particular person. Recognition of a partnership is not something we do once and for all with a ceremony or legal document. It is rather something we do over and again as we recognize the gift of that particular relationship day by day. In reference to interpersonal relationships it might be possible to say that a family is not necessarily a partnership, but it might become one by building on the given relationship. A working relationship is not necessarily a partnership, but might become one by building on the givenness of being put together and the sharing of tasks. A friend is not necessarily a partner but may become one by developing the givenness of proximity, shared task, and mutual trust. A partner is never fully a partner, but may become more fully one as proximity, sharing of task and mutual trust give way to an overplus of love in which the relationship comes together.

The fact that partnerships *happen* and cannot be defined exactly, either on a sociological or on a theological level, points us to an important theological clue in divine/human relationships. *Partnerships are a gift of God and are themselves gifted by God.* It is the *koinōnia*-creating presence of Christ that makes partnership among Christians possible. By the gift of God's grace we, who are neither worthy nor able to form mutual relationships with God and one another, discover the power to love and be loved. In this setting love and commitment shared on behalf of others is multiplied so that partnership not only happens as a gift in our lives but also the gifts appear that make growth in unity possible. As Paul says in I Corinthians 12, it is the multiplicity of God's free gifts, or *charismata,* that makes unity possible. According to Ernst Käsemann,

> like entities can only cancel each other out and render each other superfluous, unlike entities can perform mutual service and in this service of agape can become one.[31]

The *charismata* are gifts of the Spirit in the New Age; what Paul calls "first fruits" or signs in Rom. 8:23. These gifts are to be exercised through service in proportion to the gifts received. In a general sense *charismata* are a favor, capacity, truth, or endowment shared by human persons because of divine grace. In a particular sense they are the specific abilities used for the well-being, growth, and mission of the community. Every Christian possesses some of them with varying degrees of fullness and every Christian is offered the highest gifts of all: faith, hope, and love (Rom. 12:6; I Cor. 13).[32]

Looking at I Corinthians 12, we see that the variety of gifts, nevertheless, are based on the unity of their source, so that even the chaotic community at Corinth can find both unity and diversity. Because there is *One Spirit* all the spiritual gifts have the same source (I Cor. 12:4–11). Because there is *One Person* all the gifts are for building up the risen body of Christ to which all those baptized into Christ's death and resurrection belong (vs. 12–13; Eph. 4:11–16). Because the *One Ministry* is that of Jesus Christ, all the particular responsibilities are unified in that service (I Cor. 12:27–31). *Charismata* are gifts of God which give persons no grounds for boasting. In fact, Paul points out in his metaphor of the parts of the body that the highest honor is given the least honorable parts, all of which are joined together (vs. 14–26).

God's free gifts are eschatological signs of God's intention for unity among all humanity in New Creation. As such they point to God's intention that we become partners with God and others as signs of God's utopia at work. Churches can provide an abundance of examples of this understanding of partnership as a gift of God and as gifted by God. Unfortunately, however, God's "utopian intention" seen in Baptism and Communion in the church is often contradicted by the life-style of a particular Christian community.

One example of the changing pattern of partnership and the multiplication of God's gifts for service can be seen in the story of Koinonia Farm, founded by Clarence Jordan in 1942 near Americus, Georgia.[33] Jordan hoped to create a Christian farming community that would exemplify racial reconciliation and explore patterns of productive farming while following the life-style of *koinōnia* in the New Testament. Living as closely as possible by the teaching of the Sermon on the Mount led to many hard years of witness amid racial strife, so that only two families remained in 1968. Then new arrivals began to help rebuild the community and they established Koinonia Partners, Inc., and the Fund for Humanity.

> The word partners, partners, just kept hitting us time and time again because it speaks of an upward reach and an outward reach.[34]

Koinonia Partners are alive and well today, with from fifty to sixty persons living and working as partners with one another and with their neighbors in Georgia, in the United States, and around the world. The most "valuable product" is not development of farming, production, marketing, and housing, but the community that makes the work possible.[35] The center of their partnership is Christ, and its development is clearly a result of the use of God's gifts in mutual commitment, common struggle, and service to the wider community. In the midst of change the gifts were multiplied so that the partnership continually responded to new needs.

Inequality and Koinonia

A second clue that is derived from our understanding of partnership as God's eschatological gift of unity in service and the variety of *charismata* that make this possible is that *partnership does not have to do with equality of gifts.* Our partnership with God clearly does not involve an equality of gifts. Yet God has created us and invited us to become covenant partners. Our partnership with other human beings also does not involve equality of gifts. Although all of humanity is equally loved and therefore equal in God's sight, God's gifts are not distributed equally or in like manner, nor are they equally valuable for any particular task. Partnership seems to have more to do with unity in diversity of gifts than with sameness.

In their present position of inequality in church and society, women and other subordinated groups are rightly struggling to establish the fact that partnership means *equal* partnership. Women maintain that roles played and the gifts and talents contributed should not be predetermined either by biological sex or by a socialization process that stereotypes masculine and feminine roles and characteristics, placing more value on so-called "masculine roles." The liberation of both women and men to form new and creative partnerships in community depends on this struggle, for it is only the oppressed who can search out their own journey to freedom, and in the process draw the oppressor group into a mutual search for liberation.

Yet our own experiences and an abundant literature on man/woman relationships indicate that this equality is illusory. Human sin and alienation from ourselves, others, and God seem so structured into our personal, social, political, economic, and ecclesial relationships that the oppression of another seems constantly to be the by-product of the search for fulfillment. We live only in the inauguration of the New Age that is not yet fulfilled and is known to us only in bits and pieces of wholeness and in a few gifts that point toward God's intended future. Yet perhaps we would be better guided in our mutual struggles for equality in partnership of men and women and in other partnerships if we recall some of the characteristics of *koinōnia.*

Koinōnia, the new focus of relationship in Jesus Christ, is made possible by God's free gifts. These gifts are neither distributed equally nor are they sex linked. Our physical, psychological, and cultural identity affects the way we respond to God's Spirit and the way we may exercise the gifts, yet gifts are often received by persons in such a way as to contradict the stereotypes of behavior in any particular cultural setting.

Every human partnership, of whatever kind, is based, not on equality of gifts, but on a relationship of mutual trust that allows each to find her or his own best forms of service and affirms this in others. To assume we know persons' gifts simply because we know their biological sex or race is a form of "heresy," because the Spirit works in many ways through people, and the fruits of the Spirit are found in all human beings (Gal. 5:22–23).[36]

This has been part of my own experience. My partnership in marriage was based, not simply on biology or culturally assigned roles, nor on the need of either person to be better in all things, but on mutuality of relationship in Jesus Christ. For instance, when we traveled to teach in India we shared names so that Hans was Mr. Russell when we visited people from the YWCA and I was Mrs. Hoekendijk when we visited his missionary colleagues in Indonesia.

My partnership with women, with men, and with groups has often been one in which there are different forms of equality, stemming from the gifts we valued in one another for the sake of others. In working in a team ministry in East Harlem I was partner with the janitor as we and the others worked together on children's programs and Bible study groups and each found things to contribute. Jose had only begun to study the Bible himself, but this did not inhibit his gifts at preparing crafts for the children or interpreting the Bible in Spanish. Together we multiplied our gifts on behalf of the work of the church.

It is not necessary to have any sort of mathematical equality of gifts in order to share as partners in something, because partnership involves a "third thing," a common goal around which it is organized. Thus the gifts may be seen as contributing to that goal rather than as competitive. God's gifts are not ends in themselves but are valued as means of service to others.

Recently, Robin Morgan published a book, entitled *Going Too Far,* about her life and reflections in the feminist movement. In commenting on the attitude of members of the *status quo* toward any "uppity group," she says that they always accuse that group of "going too far." But what such groups have discovered is that "there *is* no 'too far.' "

> At last we seem to understand that there *is* no "too far," that *as* we grow and change we expand the categories themselves, that we create new space, that our just expectations and visionary demands for ourselves and our children bear us forward on an inexorable tide past all the fears and the clucking tongues (even our own)—much too wonderfully far for even our own senses to realize, in this, our historical present. And there is never any turning back.[37]

There is no turning back once you are on the road to freedom. God has set us on that road. God pushes us beyond our limitations, and our response is to become what our utopian God intends for us to become—God's partners in service!

3

GOD'S SELF-PRESENTATION

In our continuing search into the meaning of God's partnership with humanity, it is important to look more closely at God's self-presentation as seen in Biblical tradition. The story of the Old Testament tells us that the self-presentation of God is linked to the discovery of personhood and identity. Godself is seen in the actions of liberation with Moses and Israel in the exodus story, and in the promise of blessing not only for Abraham and Sarah but also for all the nations—all humankind (Ex. 3:13–21; Gen. 12:1–2). That same self-presentation provides additional insight into the meaning of divine and human identity, for God is discovered as both Lord and Servant. In God's freedom for us as servant we discover that, unlike other gods who have been revealed so that women and men could serve them, the God of the Old and New Testaments is One who chooses to serve and not just to be worshiped and adored.

God's actions in serving humanity come into clear focus in and through the ways Christ re-presents God to us. God is re-presented to us in that Christ helps us to see the partnership of God as Creator, in freedom to be with us in caring and love. Christ also re-presents God as Liberator, the one who opens up the possibility of redemption and new humanity through his life, death, and resurrection. Lastly he re-presents God as Advocate, the one who knows our suffering and weakness and stands present with us.[1]

Through God's re-presentation in Christ we are drawn into the story of God's serving love, so that we in turn are called to be present to God and to others as partners in the work of re-presentation. The search for the meaning of partnership includes our own struggle to identify with the life story of Jesus of Nazareth as God's representatives. As Dorothee Soelle says, "Christ represents the kingdom of identity in which the search for personal identity is sought."[2] Through this we respond to God's invitation to become representatives of new humanity and receive the gift of *koinōnia* with God and one another.

God's self-presentation reveals the meaning of true humanity as that of servanthood or caring for others. It is toward this that we seek to grow in becoming who we are intended to become as God's utopia. The new creation becomes a reality in our lives as we experience the *koinōnia*-creating presence of Jesus Christ that sets us free for others. In order to look more closely at what this means for partnership, we will turn first to look at God's self-presentation as Lord and Servant, and then at the importance of this for us as we try to understand the relationship of partnership and hierarchy. This in turn may help us find some clues from God's self-presentation for the meaning of partnership.

LORD AND SERVANT

God is present to us as both Lord and Servant, yet this self-presentation raises problems for many people concerned with partnership. Whichever way we turn in this combination we are caught in the difficult connotations of each of the words. In the minds of many persons today they are filled with the dualistic meaning of domination/subordination or master/slave relationship of God to woman and man. Because the image of Lord has been used as a religious reinforcement of the superiority of the masters who "represent" the Lord, some want to use imagery of equality in reference to God such as Sister-Brother, rather than Mother-Father, or Lord.[3]

On the other hand, the image of servant or slave has been reinforced in Western culture as a Christian example important for those assigned to the servant role of society, and theology has provided the rationale for racism, sexism, and classism. A dualistic assignment of Christian virtues such as nonaggression, humility, and caring to women, Third World groups, and the economically disadvantaged has been exposed as a fraud, and in the process all talk of servant/slave has become suspect.

Unfortunately aspects of inequality do not disappear because we rule out the words, even though the words are important reminders and reinforcers of social reality. In respect to the dynamics of relationship between human beings and between God and humanity it may not be that the most creative way to address this problem is to rule out the words. It would seem that a more helpful approach is to look at the way Biblical tradition speaks of God and of Jesus Christ as both Lord and Servant, and to see how this paradox continues as an important factor in God's self-presentation and in our re-presentation through partnership.

God's History with Humanity

"Lord" is not an unexpected title for God in the Bible, for the word is a general expression of superiority and ownership of a person and was also used to refer to the divine ruler. In Hebrew patriarchal tradition where every husband was a *ba'al*, God was thought of as the master or ruler over all. The Hebrew for God was *Yahweh* and not Lord. When the special name Yahweh was withdrawn from common usage for fear of profaning it, *Adonai*, or "Lords," was substituted in the reading.[4] The Greek Old Testament regularly translated both *Adonai* and *Ba'al* as *Kyrios*, and also used *Kyrios* to translate Yahweh. The Revised Standard Version of the Bible follows this usage in translating *Yahweh* as LORD.

> Have you not known? Have you not heard?
> The LORD [Yahweh] is the everlasting God,
> the Creator of the ends of the earth.
>
> (Isa. 40:28)

Obviously, the use of the divine name Yahweh would eliminate the excessive use of LORD in the Biblical text, but it might raise new barriers between Jews and Christians in their shared Scriptural heritage. Also it should not eliminate the divine/human relationship in which we are created to love Yahweh with heart, soul, and might. (Deut. 4:4–5; Matt. 22:34–40.) For this relationship maintains a divine "No" against every human attempt to replace God as ruler of life.

The connotations of the word "Lord" in ancient patriarchal cultures as well as in our own anthropocentric cultures are that stronger men represent God in dominating women and other weaker men, nations, and human groupings. There are two steps that can be taken to eliminate this stress on "maleness" in relation to God.

First, we can be clear that Yahweh transcends both male and female metaphors and that God's name revealed as Yahweh is itself a verbal form. Yahweh in Ex. 3:14 is sometimes translated, "I cause to happen what will happen," and is a description of a God who promises to come and be present with Moses and the people. The same description is found in Revelation 1:8, where God is described as the Coming One:

> "I am the Alpha and the Omega," says the Lord God, who is and who was and who is to come, the Almighty.

Yahweh's transcendence does not have to be imaged predominantly as Lordship above human history.

Second, we can use inclusive language about God. Although God transcends categories of human sexuality, both male and female are made in God's image and we find both masculine and feminine images of God in the Old and New Testaments.[5] If we affirm that God is Lord, ruler, and creator of *all*, then *all* people can represent God, and not only those of a particular race, sex, or class.

In spite of its misuse, the word "Lord" is important in Biblical and church tradition and important to our understanding of the self-presentation of God who is free from us and all creation. God is beyond our manipulation, including our use of God's name and authority as justification for oppression, dominance, or destruction. Yet in the Biblical tradition God is *not only Lord but also Servant.* The paradox of our faith is that the Lord chose to serve. Our God is not one of arbitrary power, but one who chooses to be free for us, and not against us. The two images must stand together. In the understanding of God's action in history the actions of Lordship and those of servanthood have been seen together as interpretations of the one divine *oikonomia.*

In pointing to "a liberating dynamic within the historical process which is variously called Yahweh, Elohim, or Adonay," Paul Hanson reminds us that the revolutionary metaphor of servant emerged with clarity in the writings of Second Isaiah.[6] Up to this time the ideas of liberation, born out of the experience of the exodus, had been most frequently transmitted in warrior images although other metaphors were used in such passages as Hos. 11:1–9; Ezek. 34; Zech. 12:10–14. In Second Isaiah the Lord and Liberator of history is seen as one who enters history in the form of a servant (Isa. 42:1; 53:1–5). As Hanson puts it:

> The metaphor of the Servant who becomes an instrument of liberation not through a destructive show of force but through vicarious suffering is a remarkable new chapter indeed in the history of the biblical liberation dynamic. For all along its most astonishing message was that divine presence is to be discovered among the suffering and the oppressed. How appropriate now that precisely in a Suffering Servant God's saving activity is discerned.[7]

Jesus Is Lord!

One of the most ancient liturgical phrases of the church is: "Jesus is Lord" (I Cor. 12:3; Rev. 19:16). In the Greek Old Testament, Yahweh was translated *Kyrios* and the postresurrection affirmation of Jesus as *Kyrios,* or Lord, identified him with God. Jesus Christ was Lord, and not Caesar, and Christians were willing to pay for this affirmation with their lives.

Jesus' title as Lord rests on two factors: Jesus is risen and he continues to exercise the power of his love in the church and the world until the new age of liberation is completed. The earthly Jesus was called "my Lord" or "Master" by his disciples. After the resurrection he was called "the Lord," to signify his victory over sin and death and his continuing unity with God as risen Lord. Jesus did not use such a title of himself. Whether he used any self-designation of a messianic title is not clear. The Gospels record that the only references that Jesus makes in connection with his mission are to the images of Son of Man and Suffering Servant. These are used to explain his relationship to the bringing of the Kingdom of God.

"Servant of Yahweh" is used, as we have seen, in Second Isaiah as a reference to the vicarious representation and suffering of God's servant. Although Jesus is not recorded as having designated himself with this title, he seems to have preferred this image of God's re-presentation because it made clear that the power and Lordship were to be discovered in suffering service and death, and not in fulfillment of the current messianic expectations of a political victory as a means of establishing God's rule.[8]

The term "Son of Man" originally meant simply "human being," but it seems to have the meaning of an apocalyptic figure in Dan. 7:13. By the time of Jesus it was regularly used to denote a preexistent divine person who would appear at the last days, or a preexistent divine person identified with the first person at creation. According to the Gospels the earthly Jesus used this title of himself. Although the title of Christ (Messiah) had already prevailed in church usage by the time the Gospels were written, they used "Son of man" when they introduced Jesus as the speaker (Mark 8:38; 9:9; 14:62; Matt. 19:28).

Jesus was familiar with the Old Testament idea that the day of the Lord's victory over evil would come in connection with a heavenly being called the Son of Man. There would be a gathering of the elect, the Last Judgment, and the end of the world (Dan. 7:9–14). Jesus claimed that his coming was directly related to this final victory of God's Kingdom. It is not known whether Jesus or Mark used the title to refer to Jesus' heavenly work as the bringer of judgment and as the representative of all the nations of people (Matt. 25:31–46). At any rate the Gospels indicate a transformation of the title to include the image of the Suffering Servant as well, so that it referred to Jesus' earthly works of healing and of humiliation and suffering on behalf of humankind (Mark 2:10; 8:27–33; 10:45).[9]

The same imagery underlies Paul's discussion of the First and Second Adam in I Cor. 15:45–47 and Rom. 5:12–21, although Paul does not make use of the "Son of Man" title.[10] Perhaps the most important text for our understanding of God's re-presentation in Christ as both Lord and Servant is Phil. 2:5–11. Here, in what is probably an early Christian liturgical hymn, Paul brings together the title of Lord with the imagery of the heavenly representative who does his work through obedient suffering. Jesus is declared to be the one who is already in the form or image of God, and yet takes upon himself the image or form of humanity in becoming a slave. The first human beings were created in the image of God and lost their ability to express this image because of their disobedience in grasping for equality in the exercise of Lordship. As Oscar Cullmann puts it:

> Already then he was the highest possible being in his relationship with God—a perfect image or "reflection" of God, as Paul attests elsewhere. But now, because of his obedience, complete equality with God in the exercise of divine sovereignty is added.[11]

In Jesus' ministry Lordship and Servanthood were together in the "establishment of justice through suffering."[12] The symbols of slavery or servanthood, so often used in the New Testament, continue to evoke strong images and experiences of domination and involuntary subordination. Yet the scandal of the words is at the heart of the Gospel story (Matt. 23:11). A Lord who voluntarily became a servant, who suffered out of love for others, has called us to do likewise.[13] The whole story of the New Testament revolves around this theme. Hoekendijk sums this up in saying:

> Now, at last, someone has come *not* to be served. That would be an old story; that we know. But *He came to serve.* Everything that was done by this Son of Man (Mark 10:45) who came to serve, including humiliation, self-emptying, *cross,* and death is summarized in one final communiqué of eight letters: *diakonia.*[14]

From this discussion we can only conclude that neither Lord nor Servant can be removed from our description of God's self-presentation, and that the key to understanding them is to allow them to remain together in the liberating paradox that witnesses to the story of God's *oikonomia.* The words cannot be separated if they are to be understood without leading to false dualisms and false uses of power. The meaning of God's Lordship in Jesus Christ is clear only in relation to the purpose of that Lordship, which is service. The purpose of God's service and subordination in Jesus Christ is to establish the Lordship of God's love.

PARTNERSHIP AND HIERARCHY

God's self-presentation as Lord and Servant can aid us in the difficult process of overcoming our own dualistic hierarchies that so often undermine the possibility of partnership. No one is ever mathematically equal with others. There is a way, however, of treating each person as a subject by encouraging the formation of dynamic power relationships, rather than static hierarchies that turn persons into objects of manipulation. This way does not pretend that power, as the ability to actualize decisions, is absent from human relationships. Rather, it claims that in nonstereotypic or nonauthoritarian settings, the exercise of power can move from one person or group to another according to the particular activity or goal. A person with clear leadership ability in one setting may become a follower in another.

The gifts of God are not equally distributed, but different gifts are needed and emerge in different settings. We will not be able to discover these gifts unless we abandon stereotyped roles and relationships that assume only those who are appointed and given structural authority have any leadership ability. Just as Lordship and Servanthood are always in a dynamic paradox in God's self-presentation in Christ, human power relationships must be in the same paradoxical tension in our partnerships. Those who form partnerships as Christians know that they are set free to live *now, as if* they were fully empowered by their Lord to live out their full human potential in the New Age. At the same time they actualize this empowerment in his life-style as *diakonia*.

Self-Identity and Power

Power and self-identity and worth are important to human partnerships, but can they be incorporated into partnership relationships without hierarchy? Some would argue that they cannot, because all human life and nature itself are arranged in forms of hierarchy and depend on certain organizations of power for preservation. Yet human beings are not solely determined by nature. They are able to go beyond themselves and nature. In the *already, not yet* of present eschatological existence, they struggle with the dimensions of human sin that cause misuse of power. At the same time, as Christians they know that they have been set free from the power of sin by Christ so that they can live in relationships where power is not necessarily destructive.

Others argue that we must do away with all hierarchy and leadership in order to be truly partners. This, it would seem, does not take into account the fact that human organization always involves power dynamics and that these are likely to be more destructive when they are not recognized and channeled constructively toward a common goal. Often those who consider themselves powerless are not able to deal constructively with power by seeing it in relation to the ability to accomplish tasks and take responsibility. Feeling helpless themselves, they claim not to want power. Viewing it as the opposite of powerlessness, they think of power as the ability to be coercive rather than coerced, potent rather than impotent, and free rather than trapped.[15] This mirror image is a distortion of the reality of the constructive alternative to powerlessness, which is empowerment for the service of others. As Jean Baker Miller reminds us in *Toward a New Psychology of Women:*

> One of the major issues before us as a human community is the question of how to create a way of life that includes serving others without being subservient. How are we to incorporate this *necessity* into everyone's development and outlook?[16]

Such a way has been blocked in the past by assigning serving functions only to women and other groups dominated because of race or class. A social pattern of what Miller calls *permanent inequality* is formed so that those of the subservient group think of themselves as lacking self-identity or worth, and are considered incapable of becoming equal. This social pattern has made it difficult for us to know how to deal with relationships of *temporary inequality* such as those between parent and child or teacher and student. Yet it is this relationship of temporary inequality, in which we learn how to maintain a dynamic tension of changing power relationships in the midst of growth, that is a key to partnership.

The revolution of consciousness that is helping women and men to see the variety of roles possible in partnerships and within persons may allow for a shift in relationships so that partnerships are made up of growing persons who are able to take responsibility both for decision-making and for carrying out decisions.[17] Women, whose psychic organizing principles have always been considered "unreal" because their selfhood comes from serving others' needs and developing human ties, may be able to contribute their strengths to total social reality.[18]

In doing so, their "weakness" might now be shared among both women and men as "strengths" of vulnerability, weakness, and helplessness so that partnerships could be made up of more whole human persons.[19]

As Paulo Freire reminds us in *Pedagogy of the Oppressed,* this new possibility of self-identity enables persons to experience and to see power as the possibility of self-affirmation together with the affirmation of others rather than a means of controlling and destroying the power of others.[20] In this setting, conflict, which is part of the interpersonal dynamics of all human beings, could be channeled into give-and-take for creative growth. Transeunce can then result in feedback that helps us toward continued self-redefinition and change.

As Miller says, "all life is conflict," but when the dominant group forces its definition of reality on the others, there is only "rigged conflict" in which the subordinates, by definition of being subordinate, cannot win.[21] In static hierarchical relationships "creative conflict" almost never happens because conflict is suppressed and ignored by the dominant persons until it explodes destructively. Self-identity includes the power for self-actualization as a subject, and not just as an object of manipulation. The key to that productive use of power in partnership is the ever-changing dynamic balance of empowerment and service in human relationships.

Service in Christian Community

In Christian communities where the *koinōnia*-creating presence of Christ makes possible partnerships in service, the self-presentation of God reminds us that all members of the community are empowered for service and not only the women or, perhaps, the clergy (Matt. 20:25–28). As Rosemary Ruether puts it:

> The principles of Christian community are founded upon a role transformation between men and women, rulers and ruled. The ministry of the Church is not to be modeled on hierarchies of lordship, but on the *diakonia* of women and servants, while women are freed from exclusive identification with the service role and called to join the circle of disciples as equal members.[22]

Such service in the New Age is possible, for all persons find their primary identity not in their assigned sex, race, or class, but in Jesus Christ who sets them free for service. In the words of Martin Luther, a Christian is "perfectly free, lord of all, subject to none," yet "perfectly dutiful servant of all, subject to all."[23]

Diakonia, the acceptance of someone else's life project as our own scenario or story, begins with accepting Jesus' own story as our own and then extends to solidarity with others. Acts 6:1–6 makes it clear that the early church saw the deacon as a "waiter on tables." Certainly *diakonia* was (and still is) a word without much glamour. Hoekendijk describes it as: "Functioning as a waiter, that is, to be subordinate, to be inconspicuous, to be available, ready to give a hand."[24] Paul uses *diakonos* once in Phil. 1:1 in reference to the work of bishops and deacons on the collection for the Jerusalem church. Aside from that, deacons are his helpers and co-workers in evangelism (both women and men).

Luke gives us the clearest description of *diakonia* in his account of Jesus' calling to ministry in Luke 4:18–19. In these simple lines Luke tells us that Jesus used a prophetic call from Isa. 61:1–2 to describe the meaning of his baptism to *diakonia:* he is anointed to preach good news to the poor . . . to set at liberty the oppressed (the crushed one; the broken victims); and in his ministry the New Age has already arrived. These words describe the calling of each of us in the New Age of liberation; a calling that was and is not easy. His *diakonia* is full of tension. God has come to be with us and, therefore, there is hope. Yet all of us know the tension of that hope-in-action which represents the impossible possibility of obedient action in service or ministry. In Jesus it is already *possible:* the lame do walk, the blind do see. God's salvation has already come and there is good news. Yet even in Jesus' own ministry, it was *not yet possible.* The signs of the New Age are already there, but so are the signs of risk, defeat, and cross which indicate that there is still more to come (Phil. 2:5–11).

Christian community is *koinōnia:* a partnership of discipleship modeled on servanthood and not on hierarchical structures of domination and subordination (John 13:1–17).[25] Its strength and power come from the power of self-actualization for others, not from selfishness. Leadership gifts that emerge are functional and not for status. Such gifts shift as a particular expertise is needed.[26] The implication of this is that churches seeking to live out their partnership in Christ may need to rethink their understanding and practice of ordination and ministry, as we shall see in Part II.

Leadership is needed in Christian communities as in other human communities, but not necessarily leadership in a fixed hierarchical model.[27] Churches are likely to grow toward partnership among their members when there is a dynamic of *leadership behavior* among a variety of people and not just one leader. James Ramey describes this form of leadership:

> Leadership behavior is behavior that permits and promotes the growth of the group in a shared direction, thereby lending status to the leader in direct proportion to the degree and value of . . . active participation and demonstration of . . . capacity to cooperatively guide the group to successful achievement of its goals.[28]

Interestingly enough, in the earliest Christian communities the concept of leadership as such did not have great emphasis. The stress of Jesus was on service in both word and life-style and not on leadership. Paul mentions leadership as "administration" only once in listings of spiritual gifts, and places it at the end of the list with "speakers in tongues" (I Cor. 12:28). The reason is not that Paul thought equality was a "principle of church order."[29] It is that leadership is clearly identified with service, and considered derivative from the leadership of Christ. Another word used by Paul of those providing administrative guidance in the church is *oikonomia* (household management): the stewardship of the gospel and of God's plan of salvation in the life of the churches. Paul says: "This is how one should regard us, as servants of Christ and stewards of the mysteries of God" (I Cor. 4:1).

In Christian communities leadership behavior that is shared among various persons for the purpose of service may become a gift that is multiplied by the one whose Spirit makes service possible. Thus in the world church partnership in development depends on recognition of the gifts of the many nations and churches involved, and not just on material aid. This shared approach contributes to *human* development so that the partnership includes persons on the way to self-actualization rather than simply those who "give and receive." Development in this sense would be understood as growth toward self-reliance, economic sufficiency, social justice, and human well-being.[30] Partnership among churches of different racial backgrounds depends on mutuality in common service so that the various participants can join together as equal partners in relation to an agreed-upon task.[31]

When there is no mutual sharing and recognition of the gifts of ministry then the *koinōnia* is likely to break down into dichotomies of black/white, rich/poor, male/female, clergy/laity. By remembering the self-presentation of the One we represent, we may be able to maintain the dynamic tension of empowerment for service and thus grow in the common relationship of partnership in Jesus Christ.

CLUES FROM GOD'S SELF-PRESENTATION

God's saving actions in history reveal God as free from us as liberating Lord and yet free for us as compassionate Servant. In responding to this self-presentation of God in Christ, we find ourselves drawn into the same paradox of *freedom from and for.* Set free in Christ, we are nevertheless called to service of our neighbor, and it is out of this empowerment for service that partnerships happen. This reflection leads us to two clues related to the fact that *koinōnia* and *diakonia* are inseparable: each provides the context in which the other may happen.

The Context of Service Is Partnership

The first clue is that there is no service without partnership, from the perspective of the Christian faith. God serves because God has chosen to be our covenant partner. We serve because God has served us and made us partners with all humanity. Genuine service involves solidarity with those being served and a willingness to be served as well as to serve. It is the process of partnership that makes service possible as a reciprocity of shared gifts. The affirmation of the other as a self-actualizing subject who can share in decision-making is basic to human growth and relationships. This can be seen in all manner of partnerships including ones between parents and children, between teachers and students, between medical professionals and patients. An example of this partnership is the personal, social, and medical care for the dying provided by centers in the Hospice Movement.[32]

The discovery of partnership or solidarity as a context for service was made in the work of members of the Church of the Saviour in Jubilee Housing, Inc., in Washington, D.C. When the project was initiated, the most difficult questions for those involved in renovating low-income housing concerned not finances and material resources, but divisions of racism and paternalism between themselves and the tenants of the slum dwellings. Only when the workers discovered ways to share stories, food, work, and life together with the tenants could they begin to discover a way to mutual service in solidarity and, therefore, in community.[33]

In such experiences of solidarity we find another aspect of God's eschatological arithmetic. *Diakonia* practiced in a context of partnership is a service of *calculated inefficiency!* Those who have gifts to share or positions of influence or authority know that they can only be partners when these gifts are shared in such a way that they continue to allow space for others to grow. Those who serve in the context of partnership in Christ's name find themselves in a *minus situation.* In order to provide space for others, they must be willing to be worked out of a job, and open to changes of agenda. In such a relationship everyone is more vulnerable, because weakness and strength are shared in common tasks. Persons or groups that are less able have to risk their talents and to share in responsibility for the common agenda if they are to grow in their ability to serve. Those persons or groups supposedly trained in service will find their professionalism, efficiency, and productivity under question, but they may in turn have a means of greater "productivity" in human lives.[34]

Diakonia in this style is practiced not according to a preconceived blueprint or ideology put together by those who "know the answers," but by a sharing of life projects of others as our own. In so doing, we become a part of God's love affair with the world; a love affair full of inefficient instruments for God's purpose: human beings, for instance, like those in a slave community or a tiny nation, or a certain humble rabbi. When we look at the way God works, we know that God's power and lordship is other than that of the "Gentiles."

> You know that those who are supposed to rule over the Gentiles lord it over them, and their great men exercise authority over them. But it shall not be so among you; but whoever would be great among you must be your servant. (Mark 10:42–43)

We can live with this calculated inefficiency for two reasons. First, we live in the anticipation of God's future and we know that even small signs are important representations of God's will for mutual partnership as the context of service. Second, we know that we will never discover the meaning of solidarity for ourselves if we do not place ourselves at the disposal of others. One person who tried this in order to develop a new life-style of partnership was John Brock. He gave up his job and became a full-time homemaker for seven months, finding out just how miserable, inferior, and dislocated he felt in order to know more about how to share in such work with his wife. Out of this experience he wrote:

> I believe that female liberation is imperative. I cannot stand by and blithely watch half a world (women) suffer because I'm not prepared to give of myself. I've tried being what much of the world (male) would say women should be and even I don't like it; and I could quite easily escape from doing "women's work." I feel if more people could endure both sides: being slave and being master, rapid changes would come as those roles were dissolved.[35]

The Context of Partnership Is Service

The second clue is like the first, for *diakonia* and *koinōnia* belong together. God is our partner because God has chosen to serve us in solidarity so that we might grow toward new humanity in Jesus Christ. Partnership is a new focus of relationship in Jesus Christ that sets us free for the service of others. Partnerships not only have a common focus but also a common agenda or life project. For Christians the common focus is Christ and the common agenda is service. This agenda involves Christians in self-actualization in relation to the needs of others as well as ourselves; a sharing of God's concern for the outcast and needy of society (Matt. 25:31–46).

The function of partnership is not *subordination but service.* Partial people who dominate or subordinate themselves in relation to others may form complementary relationships, but they will not become mutual partners unless the subordination is mutual and in a temporary and changing pattern. Partnerships grow as persons maintain a dynamic tension of leadership, responsibility, and serving so that there is a sharing of their own life projects and those of others and the gifts shared may be multiplied.

In their position of subordination in church, family, and society, it is no wonder that women strongly resist the implication that partnership involves the calling of God into communities of service or ministry. Ministry itself is a problem because it has become identified with clergy status and lost its essential connection to the function of *diakonia* as the work of the whole people of God. It is the whole people who join in carrying out the One Ministry of the One who came to serve and to give his life a ransom for many (Mark 10:45).

Even ministry as service is a special problem for women because they are almost always expected to become servants: to accept a role that has long been assigned to them in church and society. Too long the word "service" has been debased so that we think of servanthood as a means of becoming a "doormat." We identify it with *involuntary* subordination or servitude to husband, children, boss, clergy. Along with those who maintain the oppressive structures of the church, we have quickly forgotten that voluntary servanthood is, for those who receive the gift of new self-identity and freedom in Christ, the way we are empowered to serve God and others.

I experienced the function of partnership as service in seventeen years of shared ministry with oppressed people of an economic and racial ghetto in New York City. Those most oppressed, subordinated, and dehumanized by lack of employment, poverty, crime, and racism, those who were "nobodies," found that they were "somebodies" as part of a community that encouraged their ministry to others. In actions of service they came to know themselves as empowered to be human beings, able to care and to act for others and, therefore, for themselves.

In our continuing struggle to express partnership in authentic models of voluntary *diakonia* we need to discover that voluntary service is not powerlessness but empowerment that comes as a gift to those who are willing to risk giving their lives with one another in the ministry of Jesus Christ. This form of service is the expression of liberation. For the alternative to subordination is not domination but service, being set free to be ourselves for others.

God's freedom from us and for us has given us many theological clues about the meaning of partnership with God and with one another. In order to test out these clues in various situations of partnership we turn now to ways in which we might seek to live our partnerships with others in the light of God's intended future.

PART II

PARTNERSHIP WITH OTHERS

We have been looking at "Partnership with God" in order to gain clues and insights into the nature of partnership. Such a view draws our attention beyond ourselves toward God's intended future for all humanity. Yet, when we reflect on our own participation with God as stewards and servants of the New Creation, we discover that we are a part of a host of persons with whom we share hope and life.

Who are our partners? Who are the persons in our lives with whom the gifts of God's service are multiplied like loaves and fishes? Each of us has to answer this for ourselves, but there are two things that already are clear about our answers. One is that asking this question is very important. It is not necessary to pull up all partnerships by the roots and question them until they wither. But it is necessary to count our blessings and to open our eyes to the fact that God has placed us in many partnerships that provide a living network in our lives.

Secondly, whether old or young, single or married, heterosexual or homosexual, members of a larger communal group or a nuclear family unit, or whatever, we are born, live, and die in relation to other people. It is up to us to recognize the giftedness of many of these relationships so that we can nurture them into partnership, and to recognize the sickness of other relationships so that we can exercise responsible freedom with ourselves and others in seeking to renegotiate or to end them. An important aspect of partnership is the intentionality, vulnerability, and hope that come from recognizing the interdependence we have in a variety of partnerships.

As we look at partnership with others from the other end, we

79

are involved in a new focus of relationship for others that is not simply conditioned by biology, sociology, psychology, culture, or ecclesiology. Jesus seems to make this clear in that strange little story in Luke 11:27–28. A woman compliments Jesus by blessing the reproductive organs of his Mother: "Blessed is the womb that bore you, and the breasts that you sucked!" Jesus' answer is simple, "Blessed rather are those who hear the word of God and keep it!" Here and in Matt. 12:46–50 Jesus is not putting down his mother and family, but only pointing out that in the New Age it is not biology, but living out the gospel message that is the basis of relationships.

God has called us to freedom in communities of service. This calling is expressed in many ways with many persons. As we try to analyze how we respond to God's call to be partners with others we will look at some key contexts in which we might need to rethink our stewardship of partnership in relation to sexuality, ecclesiology, ministry, and education. These are by no means the only areas that might be used to test out our theological reflections in our experience, but they represent a starting point for discussion that could extend far beyond here into: legal and professional teams; parents and children; citizens and elected officials; labor and management; national economies and multinational corporations.

In all these contexts we will be exploring and testing out the clues discovered in the discussion of partnership with God, asking about their meaning in a particular relationship. All the clues are derived from the freedom of God for us and from us. God's freedom for us is discovered in God's willingness to serve us and to invite us to become partners with Christ in service. From this aspect of God reaching out to us we have discovered: that quality and not quantity is a key element in service; that service and not sexuality is the most important key to God's intended purpose for humanity; and that service of God is not a form of subordination but of empowerment. In God's freedom from us we discover that God's reality is not necessarily ours, and the arithmetic of partnership is not that which we expect: the whole is greater than the sum of the parts; the gifts of the Spirit are not equally distributed; and calculated inefficiency is often the way partnership grows through grace.

4

ESCHATOLOGY AND SEXUALITY

In the discussion of partnership with others we must return to the question of who we are as addressed by God to become what God intends. Chapters 2 and 3 have sketched out the conviction that God intends us to become partners in service; sharing the work of Christ for others. If this is God's utopia, how do we make sense of human sexuality? In understanding partnership primarily in the eschatological dimension of New Creation, we still must work out an ethic of sexuality that can inform our views of human relationships.

In the past, eschatology has often had a negative influence on the Christian understanding of human sexuality. Although the Biblical creation story cannot be said to indicate that sexuality is the bearer of the image of God, it certainly does indicate that the image is both male and female and that this is good (Gen. 1:27–31).[1] In contrast to this, the Biblical understanding of New Creation is often understood as a fulfillment in which sexuality and sexual pleasure are excluded.[2] Paul's teachings in I Corinthians that celibacy is the preferable state of life in view of the end times is overshadowed by his stress on the fact that all relationships, even celibacy, are *hōs mē,* put under the call of Christ to mission and service.[3] Just as God can be imaged as male and female yet transcends all such images, human beings are both male and female, but also transcend themselves toward full humanity.

Rather than necessarily leading to a negative attitude toward human sexuality, eschatology can provide a key for overcoming the limited views of past centuries that linked sexual identity and roles with "biological determinism." Eschatology may be able to free us to hear the discoveries of natural science as shedding light on the possibilities of New Creation, rather than as threatening our images of Old Creation. In my view this would not be an apocalyptic eschatology in which one is concerned about sexuality because the end time is near, but an adventology in which God's New Creation is coming into our lives now, bringing the dimension of the holy into the everyday dynamics of human interaction and expectancy.

Tom Driver has pointed out that the next step to be taken in discussing the meaning of human sexuality lies in the realm of eschatology.

> For too long, the question Christian moralists have asked about sex is, what shall we not do? The real question to ask, about sex as about all other ethical matters, is: For what may we hope?[4]

In an eschatological view of sexuality the self-identity of a person is rooted in biological gender and developed into gender identity and roles, but finds a new focus of relationship in Jesus Christ that sets persons free for others. In order to see how *koinōnia* and *diakonia* are thus related to sexuality we will begin with a description of what is understood by human sexuality and then turn to see how this is expressed in various styles of partnership. Finally we will look at how clues from God's utopia illuminate the relationship of eschatology and sexuality.

MEANING OF HUMAN SEXUALITY

There are many descriptions of human sexuality, and no one description can catch all the perspectives on what is so basic to the mystery of our existence. A provisional working description used here is: *an ever-evolving sense of self-identity rooted in, but not determined by, one's biological sex.* Wholesome sexuality fosters intrapersonal and extrapersonal growth toward integration according to the study on *Human Sexuality* by a task force of the Catholic Theological Society of America.[5] It includes generative and genital functions, but is far broader than these in its reference to whole human persons.

The study speaks of it as "the way of being in, and relating to the world as a *male* or *female* person."[6] Norman Pittenger underlines the transeunt quality of sexuality in saying that it is what makes interpersonal relationships possible. He sees sexuality "as the bodily, physiological-psychological-emotional base or ground" for the capacity to love and a way of loving.[7]

New Perspectives on Sexuality

The "sexual revolution" in Western society took place in about the first fifty years of the twentieth century. It was marked by a dramatic loosening of sexual attitudes and activities due to scientific studies of sexuality, medical advances, emancipation of women, and erosion of religious and social taboos.[8] Debates taking place now in the life of the churches are not part of the "sexual revolution" as such but are rather an attempt to catch up to society at large and to seek to provide moral guidance in a changed setting.

In this changed setting the perceptions of sexuality are very much confused in people's minds. Sexual liberation is falsely identified with women's liberation and human liberation. Much of what has happened in the sexual revolution has led to the further dehumanizing of women as exploited sex objects.[9] Sex has been turned into an economic commodity and the entire culture has been more and more eroticized through the use of sex to sell consumer products. When this corruption of human sexuality is challenged by groups such as those related to women's liberation, there is great resistance to reexamination of the values involved. Those who do not accept the standards set by the white, heterosexual male culture are perceived as a threat to the identity of this culture even though they are raising key issues for *all* persons. The church reflects the anxiety of this situation, so that the issues over which it exercises great emotion are not those of war, economic exploitation, racism, poverty, and the like. Rather, the most controversial issues are those of birth control, abortion, women's ordination, and gay liberation —issues that challenge previously accepted cultural and religious views of human sexuality.[10]

In our discussion of human sexuality it is important to keep the working descriptions of words we are using clearly in mind in order to avoid confusion. The word "sex" is usually used in English to refer to genital behavior. *Sexuality* refers to the whole range of behaviors that go into our makeup as male and female.[11] According to the preliminary study on *Human Sexuality* of the United Church of Christ,

> sexuality is a central dimension of each person's selfhood, but it is not the whole of that selfhood. It is a critical component of each person's self-understanding and of how each relates to the world.[12]

Sexism is an ideology expressed in hidden or overt attitudes or actions that assign one sex to an inferior status or worth. Sexism reinforces false stereotypes of what masculine and feminine roles must be and operates in a system that punishes those who deviate from these norms such as "uppity women" or "effeminate men." Our sexist attitudes lead to a preoccupation with women as genital sex objects used to satisfy male needs for pleasure or procreation.

Sexism leads to *heterosexism,* an ideology that assigns a person to inferior status and lack of human dignity because his or her sexual orientation is toward persons of the same sex.[13] The major reinforcer of systemic heterosexism in our culture is male homophobia, the fear of homophiles or those who love others of the same sex. Androcentric society has long divided human sexuality into a masculine/feminine duality and maintained the privileges of males by projecting their weaknesses on women. One way to perpetuate the subordination of women is to punish any men whose behavior can be labeled as female.

Human beings are born with a *biological sex* as a result of the combination of chromosomes (XX for female and XY for male). Both chromosomal embryos have the potential to develop either male or female genitalia and structures. The embryos will all become females unless in the sixth week the male embryo (XY) "instructs" the gonads to differentiate as testicles rather than ovaries and then hormones secreted cause male development.[14] Unless something goes wrong with this development, it is possible to declare that a child at birth is biologically male or female.

An infant does not develop a core *gender identity* until sometime between eighteen months and three years. According to the report presented by the United Presbyterian General Assembly's Task Force to Study Homosexuality, the psychological conviction that one is female or male is believed to be determined by the interplay of "prenatal hormonal setting of neural tissues or some other kind of prenatal biological 'disposition'; and post-natal socialization and learning."[15] The most important factor according to most scholars at present is psychosocial.

Beyond age three the *gender role* of the child and developing adult remains flexible. The role develops according to the ongoing psychosocial influences that help to define for each person what sorts of actions, thoughts, and self-identity are associated with being female or male in a particular culture. Different people associate different roles with threat to their basic gender identity. A role, according to Janet Chafetz, is defined sociologically as "a cluster of socially or culturally defined expectations that individuals in a given situation are expected to fulfill."[16] Gender role definitions are subject to change, but not gender identity. Human sexuality as an evolving sense of self-identity would seem to include a person's sense of gender identity as well as gender role and sexual orientation.[17]

A lot of theology in the past has discussed human sexuality under the guise of what is biologically "natural." Such discussion often turns out to be rather uninformed about present biological studies of human development and tends to read long-held theological doctrines into the discussion without reexamining new biological, sociological, or psychological perspectives. For instance, heterosexuality has been the "natural norm" in society. Yet studies by Alfred C. Kinsey and others have shown that heterosexuality and homosexuality are not necessarily exclusive. Probably only about ten percent of either end of the scale are exclusively homosexual or heterosexual according to the Kinsey studies. The rest of us are bisexual. Not only are we capable of becoming either male or female as embryos, but also most of us are capable of a wide variety of sexual behavior, as seen in other cultures.[18]

In relation to the psychology of sex roles there has been a marked change in the traditional views. This is spelled out in the United Church of Christ report on *Human Sexuality.*[19]

1. The extent of psychological sex differences between women and men is not as large as was assumed. Men appear to develop more visual/spatial and mathematical skills and are more aggressive. Women appear to develop more verbal skills. Some of these differences may be attributed to the way children are treated and educated.

2. The psychological sex differences are biologically based in part, but are highly trainable and influenced by environment.

3. Psychological needs in human development indicate only that an accurate self-classification of one's gender is needed, but there is no need to have particular masculine or feminine traits except because of societal pressure.

4. Few people fail to develop an accurate self-classification of gender (one to two percent), and psychological handicaps are likely to develop if persons develop *only* sex-appropriate traits.

5. Psychological sex differences and sex identity do not account for women's and men's different and unequal social roles. Such roles appear to be culturally assigned and then labels are attached to certain roles and to certain expressions of sexual orientation.

The evidence from biology, psychology, and sociology continues to change so that those concerned to understand human sexuality need to remain open to new evidence and to be aware that there is always a spectrum of opinions regarding such matters. Nevertheless, it is not natural science, either that of the Hebrews or the Greeks or that of the twentieth century, that should form Christian theological and ethical perspectives on sexuality. The source of theological reflection on God's purpose for new humanity must be our faith in Jesus Christ as it is interpreted through critical reflection on Biblical and church tradition. This in turn needs to be informed by empirical sciences and addressed to the questions and situations of contemporary society. Such a procedure can be seen in the reports on *Human Sexuality* of the United Church of Christ and the Catholic Theological Society of America.[20]

Biblical Views of Sexuality

For the purposes of our reflection on partnership it is important to look at the way an eschatological approach to human sexuality might illuminate Biblical interpretation of human sexuality and human interrelationships. We turn first to Biblical views and then to an interpretation of these views in the light of God's intention of *koinōnia* between persons.

Perhaps the most significant Old Testament statement about sexuality is one that was discussed in Chapter 2 in relation to the image of God. Not only in Genesis, but elsewhere in the Old

Testament, there is evidence of *gynomorphic* as well as *andromorphic* images used to portray the way God relates to human beings and their concerns.[21] Female imagery such as that of the womb, according to Phyllis Trible, suggests

> a natural and spontaneous relationship between the divine and the human in contrast to one based on adoption, duty and law. It embodies God's intimate embrace.[22] (Isa. 49:15; Ps. 22:9–10)

Not only does this temper the assertion that Yahweh is a male deity, but also it expresses our understanding of divine/human relationships in which both masculine and feminine images are appropriate. At the same time, this encourages us to see that both God and human persons can be said to demonstrate a full range of capacity for relationship.

Biblical tradition is not very interested in God's sexuality except to reject fertility imagery as used in the Canaanite divine pantheon. Its focus for both God and persons is on God's covenanting action and its implications for human history. In this context there is free use of images for the motifs of blessing and salvation.[23] What is required of the people is covenant faithfulness even as God is faithful. Although Israel prefers masculine images of God, many metaphors are used to express this covenant relationship including sexual metaphors and those of marriage, of father and mother, and of harlotry.

In the light of the covenant, cultic purity is very important and sexual practices such as temple prostitution are condemned; the power of fertility is related directly to God's gracious blessing.[24] The taboos related to birth, death, sexual discharges, and uncleanness are part of the deep-seated fear of the ancients of the power of life-giving forces. Other restrictions are due to patriarchal marriage and its emphasis on the role of women in child-bearing and nurture.

The Old Testament is not concerned with sexuality as such. "It contains no doctrine of human sexuality." Rather it takes a functional view of the relationship between men and women for the purpose of mutuality and of procreation.[25] According to John McNeill, "mutual love and fulfillment are equally a biblical norm for human sexuality" along with that of procreation.[26] The principal message of the Old Testament concerning sexual morality seems to be that love, including sexual mutuality, requires responsibility for the other person through covenant faithfulness. Prohibitions of homosexuality are in this context. It was perceived as a violation of God's will because it dishonored the other by making him into a woman and resisted the command to "be fruitful and multiply" so that the seed of the father would be carried on and the nation continue (Gen. 1:28). In Gen. 38:1–11, Onan is condemned for preventing the possible conception of a male heir for his brother and thus destroying life in spilling his seed on the ground. At that time the male seed was considered the entire source of life deposited in the female to be nurtured.[27]

Gospel accounts of Jesus' life and ministry indicate that he nowhere condemns or discusses homosexual practices and, aside from his teaching on divorce, there is very little said about interrelationships based on sex or family life (Mark 10:2–12). As we shall see in the last section, marriage does not play the same role in the New Testament because it is not blood ties and progeny but the new life of those who love the Lord that is the focus of Jesus' and Paul's teachings (Mark 2:25; Matt. 12:46–50; I Cor. 7). One's personal immortality is found through participation in the Kingdom of God and all are welcome into that Kingdom, including the Ethiopian eunuch (Acts 8:26–39; Matt. 19:12). In this Biblical overview we might conclude with a summary of McNeill:

> The positive ideal concerning the use of human sexuality proposed in the New Testament is the need all human beings are under to struggle to integrate their sexual powers into their total personality, so that their sexual drive can be totally at the disposition of their desire to achieve union in love with their fellow human beings and with God.[28]

MARRIAGE AND ALTERNATIVE LIFE-STYLES

Before discussing the Biblical views of sexuality in the light of an eschatological understanding of partnership in New Creation, we need to look at the various life-styles people are trying out and the questions that these actions raise for the interpretation of marriage and other human relationships in contemporary society. For eschatological hermeneutics calls for living out the questions in the light of the Biblical message.[29]

Those who talk about changes in life-styles and marriage are not necessarily encouraging irresponsibility or promiscuity. Instead, they are responding to the social challenges of our time and seeking out responsible and moral ways of dealing with human sexuality in a modern context.[30] Marriage and childbearing and rearing are very much affected by economic, social, political, and population needs in a society, and there are various ways families and relationships between persons have been established in different times, places, and cultures.[31] In society today marriage is a "dependent variable." It does not determine the society, but very much reacts and interacts with social changes around it.

Marriage is also affected by particular religious or faith commitments which carry with them a wide variety of norms and values that influence the way women and men arrange their household patterns and life-styles. When we talk about families as an "endangered species" today, we obviously do not mean the relationship of persons in community. As reflected in the creation story and also in the psychosocial developmental studies, this need for community with others is part of what it means to be human. The patterns of community and the ways that man and woman come together are various, but they are always there. What is being endangered in both the society and in the church is the single-unit nuclear families of white, middle-class Americans.

The nuclear family of mother and father and children is becoming more and more fragile under pressures of changing social needs. In fact, it is no longer even the dominant pattern of family life in the United States. In 1974 only 37 percent of the U.S. family units were nuclear.[32] Yoshio Fukuyama has pointed out that social forces and technological change have contributed to the changing functions of the family in Western society. Formerly the family controlled sexual access; provided an orderly context for reproduction and care, nurture and socialization for children; was a context for economic activity and support; and ascribed social status. These functions are changing or being shared with other institutions or structures, and control of sexual access no longer is effective.[33] Let us look at some of these social challenges and at emerging alternative family structures.

Social Challenges to the Nuclear Family

In a rapidly changing society many pressures are converging that cause women and men to seek out alternative ways of ordering their households and developing relationships with one another and their children. Among these social challenges to the nuclear family of husband, wife, and children are the following:

First, the emergence of the postindustrial society. Since the Second World War our society, which was already postagrarian, has been becoming postindustrial. Already cybernetics makes it possible for a centralized elite to control the international economic systems and for a very few workers to produce needed industrial goods. Expanding work opportunities are more and more in the service sector of hospitals, food, teaching, social service, and welfare for the poor who are marginalized by lack of work opportunities.[34] The small family unit, necessary for mobility in industrial society, is no longer as important. The economic function of the family becomes more and more one of a consumer unit rather than of contributing to production (except by the unrecognized economic contribution of housework and family care).

In addition, the increasing pressures of society have isolated the basic family unit in the private sector and deprived it of larger support systems. At the same time, they have placed much responsibility on that unit for providing meaning, identity, and purpose in an impersonal and alienated world. The result is that the nuclear family has become a fragile social unit, frequently ending in divorce and developing a pattern of serial monogamy (one spouse at a time).

Secondly, medical advances have greatly changed the biological necessity or even desirability of bearing large numbers of children. The increase in average longevity, general health, and safety in childbearing has resulted in a worldwide population explosion. The increasing safety of contraceptives and of abortion means that women are less likely to bear children. The birthrate among Western middle-class groups is declining because of economic pressures and concern for quality of life. Yet Third World groups in the United States and abroad often face government regulations that may deny access to abortion because of poverty and yet promote genocide through sterilization programs. Thus the birthrate of the poor is regulated to provide greater access to resources for the wealthy.[35]

Thirdly, women's liberation has emerged as a movement in the United States and around the world. Middle-class women are beginning to look for meaningful expression of their talents in all sectors of society. They are questioning socially assigned roles and searching for alternatives to their roles in the modern nuclear family where they find themselves exploited through media and commercialism as sex objects and consumers. Often they can find little meaningful use of their energies for the last forty years of their lives when their children are maturing. For reasons of either economic need or equal development of their capacities, women are working outside the home. In 1976, in the United States, 55.5 percent of all women between eighteen and sixty-four were in the job pool as were 48.8 percent of mothers with children under eighteen years.[36] Many women are working to reform marriage and along with their husbands struggle toward "egalitarian marriages."[37]

Lastly, men's liberation is at least being considered by many thoughtful men.[38] Urged to take a look at their own role assumptions about identity, machismo, dominance, and the resulting fear, insecurity, heart attacks, and all the rest, men are beginning to look for more human patterns for their lives. Together with women they search for ways to share in a variety of activities and patterns, not as masculine or feminine but as human. This includes a search for alternative styles of household arrangements and more healthy atmospheres for child-rearing that provide a variety of male and female role models for the children.[39]

There are other social challenges, but the ferment and change going on within and among persons and in society mean that marriage and child care are no longer automatic things for girls to do when they grow up. It is hoped that these tasks will be chosen with much greater care, and only after as much growth and experience as possible.

Alternative Family Structures

In order to look at the many options being exercised both among church members and among members of the larger society, it is helpful to list examples of alternative family structures without making any attempt to be exhaustive.

One set of alternatives can be seen in the amazing variety of cultural and subcultural patterns that have existed all along, but have been ignored by those of us who preferred to think that our comparatively recent nuclear family pattern was normative. Cultures all over the world organize their households in extended families and various types of economic units, with women sometimes as workers and sometimes in the home; with men sometimes the head of household, and sometimes participants in the wife's household.[40] Subcultures in our own country of Native Americans, Spanish Americans, blacks, Asians, and poor whites have many varieties in their family patterns often related to survival in the face of racism and classism on the part of white, affluent society.[41]

Another type of alternative is the various communal living arrangements that have emerged as a means of developing a more balanced style of life. Some of these are economic communes based on the land, or with adults and children living together and supporting themselves through small industry. Others support themselves through the income of those who have salaried jobs. Still others are religious communities with persons living together as a sign of communal relationship for the larger community.

Still another alternative is the multi-adult household, usually of three or four adults with or without children. Such households provide economic and personal advantages with a wider number of primary relationships, but are small enough to fit into existing patterns without too much difficulty. They provide greater opportunity for adult models and relationships for children.[42]

A fourth is that of the intimate network. Here husbands, wives, and children live in separate dwelling units, but form an intimate social circle. Much of life is shared without actual sharing of house or property. An intimate network or multi-adult household can lead to a formalization of group marriage although at this time this is not recognized legally, or it can lead to nonmarital cohabitation.[43]

In nonmarital cohabitation couples live together without formal marriage ceremony either as a trial marriage or as a marriage in which they believe that two persons have more freedom to grow and less social restriction. In spite of social disapproval this often helps to avoid an early legal divorce, but it puts emotional strains on the couple and may be a poor foundation if parenting marriage is intended.

Homosexual marriage is common among same-sex couples, although it is not very often solemnized in religious ceremonies and is not recognized legally. Many such unions exist between male/male and female/female, and the separation rate among gay couples does not appear to be greater in society than the divorce rate in heterosexual marriage in the United States, which is one out of three. Those living in such arrangements may be "true" homosexuals because of their psychological sexual orientation. Others may be what McNeill calls "conditional" homosexuals because they are bisexual but have chosen to live with a person of the same sex.[44]

Singleness is another alternative life-style. Society labels persons single if they are not living in couples, yet no one is actually single because everyone lives in a variety of interrelated social patterns. Today singleness is considered a healthy and preferred option by increasing numbers of women and men. In spite of the social stigma associated with this, especially for women, many are discovering that our own personal growth, creativity, and maturity increases when we decide to live by ourselves. Wisely aware of increasing divorce rates and the difficulties of marriage, many young people postpone marriage until after they have developed their own careers. Persons are single because of divorce and often find themselves as single parents. Others are older people who find themselves single by choice or by early death of their spouse.[45]

The list could go on indefinitely. The proliferation of alternatives to what still remains the predominant style of marriage continues and James Ramey, the director of the Center for the Study of Innovative Life Styles at the Center for Policy Research in New York, already lists nine types of marriage, not to mention other life-styles.[46] In all of the above examples there are many variables that would increase the types even further. In all living arrangements one's sexuality and its expression through monogamy, polygamy, promiscuity, celibacy, heterosexual, homosexual, or bisexual activity have to be worked out in and through that pattern or life-style. Genital sex is not necessarily the category that determines the type of living arrangement, but as an important aspect of human sexuality the handling of this area of life is key to the interaction of the group involved.

All such alternative living arrangements can be entered into out of deep religious commitment or out of none. All do depend, however, on some shared value system and a common commitment to a shared agenda if the relationship is to grow toward full partnership. These arrangements are not for any one group of people, for such possibilities could be open to people of varying ages, races, cultures, or physical handicaps. And they are arrangements which like the nuclear family are not necessarily lifelong. People often relate to others in a variety of patterns during the various phases of their life either by choice or because they are forced to do so by economic, social, or personal circumstances. All the relationships, whether traditional or alternative, are dependent on the possibility of responsible commitment to growth, trust, and caring if they are to be viable and deeply human.

Many of the changes we have been discussing are already represented by large numbers of people in the United States. Family types were extremely diverse even in 1974: 37 percent were nuclear families; 11 percent were couples with no children at home; 12 percent were single-parent families; 11 percent were remarried nuclear families; 4 percent were kin networks of three generations or extended families; 19 percent were single without children; and 6 percent were emerging experimental forms such as the commune- type of family groupings.[47] Not only have our acknowledged cultural and religious values lagged behind these shifts but so have our legal codes. Changes are needed that would ease the tensions on the nuclear family, such as no-fault divorce and support from the church for those in difficulties.[48] Such changes might make it possible for the church to provide moral guidance and support for those who find their life situations so different from those of earlier centuries.

As we shall see, the teachings of Jesus and Paul on marriage and human relationships are not necessarily inconsistent with much of what women and men are seeking today through alternative models of equal partnership. Men and women who challenge the hypocrisy and destructiveness of many of our marriage customs are neither causing the social dissolution of the nuclear family nor necessarily contradicting God's intentions for human development. They are responding to hypocrisy and injustice and pointing to alternative possibilities, some of which could encourage faithfulness, love, and trust. They are saying what any social scientist can tell us. We do live in a new age created largely through human technology. This same technology threatens to destroy the planet and humanity unless countless persons begin to live now in ways that are more human and less crippling to the lives of those caught in the impersonal and competitive social patterns of our world.

SEXUALITY AND PARTNERSHIP

Today many Christians are in search of a sound theology of human sexuality that can help to make sense of the changing patterns of sexuality and the various forms of partnership. Of course, there is no one theology of sexuality,and each book and report cited, as well as those not cited, has a slightly different perspective. Here, however, I would like to look at sexuality in an eschatological perspective, beginning from the New Creation.

When we turn to look at human sexuality from the point of view of *koinōnia* we perceive sexuality as an expression of intrapersonal and interpersonal growth which is focused in a new relationship in Jesus Christ. Once we begin here and not with Genesis we are able to relate our discussion to a whole person and to allow for human development, not just in two halves, but as whole persons capable of human interrelatedness. In view of New Creation, relationship and not propagation is the key to the meaning of masculine and feminine qualities that are creatively shared for the purpose of serving others.

This image of partnership for service of *diakonia* is clear in the story of Jesus Christ, whose true humanity flowed from his relationship to the will and love of God and to others (both male and female). His teachings and life point to God's partnership with humanity in the New Age and our need to grow into life in that age where God's will is done on earth.

Eschatological Perspectives

We are God's utopia: created to become full human beings in relation to God, others, and ourselves. In human beings sexuality is *omnipresent* but not *omnipotent.* [49] What distinguishes us from animals is not genital sex or reproduction, but the ability to assign meaning to these actions. All our ways of being as male and female can be vehicles for relationships of love and growth as we develop in Christ toward a full human personhood (Eph. 4:13). But they can also be vehicles for broken relationships of hatred and alienation among persons.

In approaching New Testament *teachings on marriage* in an eschatological perspective, we must remind ourselves again that the Biblical patterns changed over the centuries and were not static. They included polygamy and extended families and did not reflect the pattern of small nuclear families. They did reflect a strong patriarchal structure in which females were honored as mothers and emphasis was on procreation for survival.

The only direct teaching of Jesus on marriage is that contained in the conflict story of Mark 10:2–12. This saying of Jesus is presented as a response to the challenge of the Pharisees and not as a new law. Jesus is challenged about the meaning of Deut. 24:1 which permits divorce of the woman by a man if she does something "objectionable." What was objectionable was a subject for debate among different schools of Pharisees. Instead of allowing himself to be drawn into this debate, Jesus points to the deepest intention of marriage as seen in Genesis 1 and 2. Marriage is a gift of God as a relationship of solidarity and loyalty for the protection of family life and the life of the community. It appears that Jesus regarded marriage as an indissoluble union in which *both* the husband and the wife have equal responsibility.

How can we interpret this passage today through the leading of the Holy Spirit? First, by recognizing that Jesus' constant concern was not the "law" itself, but going behind it to God's intention and then applying it to actual persons. Thus, for instance, in his concern to defend the disciples' plucking of corn on the Sabbath he said, "The sabbath was made for [persons], not [persons] for the sabbath" (Mark 2:27).

Secondly, Jesus and Paul viewed the social order, like the natural order, as God given in a certain pattern. This is not as we usually view social order today, as a changing construct of human organization. Yet Jesus was willing to treat each situation contextually, and with concern for the persons involved.

All things were viewed in the light of the breaking in of God's Kingdom and of the relationships of love, obedience, and integrity made possible by God's love.

Lastly, alongside this one brief conflict story in which Jesus points out the basic truth that God did not intend divorce and broken, unfaithful relationships, we have other indications that Jesus welcomed all the outsiders and sinners and reserved his sharpest criticism for those who were hypocrites in thinking about right actions and forgetting the orientation of their hearts (Matt. 5:28). If we keep in mind that marriage was made for man and woman, but not man and woman for marriage, we may be able to raise the deeper question of ways relationships between persons in our time can be supported as relationships of trust, mutuality, and responsibility.

Paul, like Jesus, follows the injunction that man and woman are not made for marriage. Both he and Jesus broke the customs of their times by refusing marriage for the sake of their work for the Kingdom of God and the good news of God's liberation. In I Cor. 7:10–31, Paul quotes Jesus' saying about divorce. Yet in his advice on marriage, divorce, celibacy, and slavery Paul is pointing toward an ethic of the New Age in which all such relationships are *hōs mē* (as if not), because they are at the disposal of the wider task of witnessing to the gospel.[50] In Christ the established orders of creation have been decisively changed so that religious, racial, and sexual differences are not lost as a basis of our self-identity, but they are not counted of ultimate significance. All are set free to be accepted as equals in Christ's church (Gal. 3:28).

The use of the metaphor of marriage in Eph. 5:21–33 to illuminate the relationship of Christ and the church continues the Old Testment understanding of marriage as a sign of the covenant relationship between God and Israel. In this sense of mutual faithfulness and sacrifice the metaphor is very powerful for understanding the meaning of covenant partnership. However, in its usage in church tradition this text has served to reinforce the model of subjection of the wives (church) to their husbands (Christ). The result is that women are tied to the structures of fallen creation through sexist attitudes, and marriage is often unable to represent a true metaphor of deep mutuality.[51]

Christian freedom stems from our justification by God's grace through faith and no outward circumstance can be said either to merit or to earn God's love, nor can it be considered a barrier to being welcomed into the fellowship of the body of Christ. Paul makes this clear in his struggles against the requirement that all male Gentile Christians be circumcised. This insistence seems to have raised as much controversy in the early churches as the issues of the ordination of woman or of homosexuals are raising in the churches of today (Acts 10–11; Gal. 2). For Paul, circumcision or no circumcision was not of ultimate importance except as it became a stumbling block for the understanding and acceptance of God's free gift of faith (I Cor. 7:17–20). Similar struggles are constantly part of church life as human beings seek out ways to restrict and control God's grace, requiring converts to become "like me" before being allowed entrance into the church.

The circumstances of Paul's time and his expectation of the Parousia never provided occasion for Paul to work out fully and consistently his teachings in regard to slave and free, male and female. Nor did they provide occasions for our particular questions of today such as: Does a "secular" person have to become "religious" in order to share in church life; or an African become "European" before being a Christian; or a homosexual become "heterosexual" before being accepted by Christ?

All these questions are pressing in on us today. The questions themselves are signs of the New Age breaking into our lives, for the Spirit of Christ is manifested in the lives of those who formerly were not "qualified" to minister among us. When God's Spirit was manifested in the life of Cornelius, the centurion, Peter was led to see that "God shows no partiality," and to baptize him (Acts 10:34; Gal. 2:6). When challenged, Peter said,

> If then God gave the same gift to them as . . . to us when we believed in the Lord Jesus Christ, who was I that I could withstand God? (Acts 11:17)

God's Utopia

The "clues from God's utopia" which were suggested in Chapter 2 have bearing here as we try to maintain an eschatological perspective on how human sexuality and the gift of partnership in Jesus Christ are interrelated. Two helpful clues were: Not sexuality but transeunce in service is the bearer of the image of God as it is expressed through various forms of partnership. The gifts of the Spirit are not equally distributed among partners.

In Jesus as the model of new humanity we see that *diakonia* is the key expression of human transeunce (or going beyond ourselves toward others) and growth toward full maturity. As the *Catholic Theological Report* puts it:

> For Christian men and women, this call for full maturity takes on an added dimension as much as we see ourselves as called to growth in Christ, our model.[52]

Tom Driver has pointed out that there is a problem with holding up Jesus as a model for human sexuality, for Jesus does not appear to have had any sexuality according to the Gospels. In church tradition this seems to have implied that sex and sin are to be identified and that Jesus overcame his human nature as a sexual being. This is not necessarily so, for celibacy does not imply that persons do not continue to act out of their centered identity as male or female. The Gospels do not speak of Jesus in this regard, perhaps because Jesus did not speak about it. This silence does not in any way deny his full humanity and full human sexuality, but rather witnesses to Jesus' own refusal to sanction the religious status of sexual taboos.[53]

In this sense, the issue of sexuality as having a divine force or power of its own, to be guarded and surrounded with religious taboos, was demythologized. Sexuality and the taboos associated with women, sex, birth, and blood were no longer considered central in God's New Age (Luke 8:43–48). In the same way Paul could treat such things as *hōs mē* because they were important as expressions of faithfulness, but were not a source of salvation in relation to new life in Jesus Christ (I Cor. 8). Jesus not only imaged servanthood as the key to full relationships in partnership with others, he also placed sexuality in the context of all faithful relationships. Perhaps in following this clue we will be more guided by Jesus' example than by ancient taboos. As Driver puts it,

> I believe that the construction of a Christian ethic of sex cannot be properly attempted as long as one retains the mythology of sex that grew up in the ancient religions, is perpetuated in new ones, and from which Jesus as the Christ would liberate us.[54]

The distribution of the gifts of the Spirit so that *koinōnia* may grow and become strong in the service of others is never equal. In the metaphor of the body, Paul reminds us that all the parts are equal in God's sight but not all parts are the same (I Cor. 12:14–31). The gifts that persons receive in order to contribute to the life of Christian communities are often overlooked because of prejudice stemming from racism, classism, sexism, or heterosexism. Yet clearly God does raise up persons from every "nation" or human grouping and often God uses those who are outcasts (those of little account) to call us back to our new focus in the gospel message of God's love.

All of us have the gift of love and that gift is expressed through our human sexuality as male and female persons. No matter what the expression of that gift, it is subject to faithful and responsible stewardship of one's life in the service of others. There are many varieties of gifts and their purpose in God's New Creation is

> . . . to equip the saints, for the work of ministry, for building up the body of Christ, until we all attain to the unity of the faith and of the knowledge of the Son of God, to mature [personhood], to the measure of the stature of the fulness of Christ. (Eph. 4:12–13)

5

ADVENT SHOCK AND THE CHURCH

As we turn to see the ways in which God's partnership with us leads us to respond as partners with God and one another, the question in the minds of many Christians is: What about partnership in the church? Where is *koinōnia* in parish churches, or in the actions of various denominations or churches in all parts of the globe? The promise is that the gift of the *koinōnia*-creating presence of Christ will be among the two or three, or two or three thousand who gather in his name (Matt. 18:20). We gather in all manner of groupings to celebrate the story of God's love and pray that God's will of love and justice be done on earth. Sometimes our actions and those of others speak louder than our prayers, declaring that the Christ whose history and life story is with the oppressed and misfits of society is not welcome (Matt. 25:31–46).

We look for partnerships of commitment, vulnerability, and trust; for those who join in a common struggle in the service of others; for those who support one another, ministering in the context of the human needs and issues of their world.[1] But we often see people dwelling in the *status quo:* either the frozen *status quo* of some other age, or the current *status quo* of alienation, domination, and dehumanization.

> There is a rumor [according to Hoekendijk] that they justify their strange activity on the ground of an emended text of Paul: "Now there remaineth faith, hope, and charity, these three, but the greatest of these is the *status quo.*"[2]

Perhaps it is sometimes difficult to recognize the church as what Ruether calls a "paradigm of liberated humanity" because it is so often preoccupied with problems of *future shock*.[3] As Alvin Toffler makes clear in his book on this topic, future shock is maladjustment with the present because of a longed-for past.[4] As with culture shock, future shock leaves persons not knowing how to cope and fearful of the unknown because they are thrust into a world where there are no familiar landmarks and customs. Habitual ways of relating to people and understanding what is going on around us no longer seem to work because people and social reality are changing.

The rapidity of change in our society leads people to cope with change by a mechanism of "culture lock" in which they hang on to the traditions or *status quo* of their parents or grandparents and expect the church to be an "enclave of the past." Others move reluctantly toward tomorrow, but their attitude is of "cultural loss" in which they are willing to update things but see this as a loss of cultural values. Others, perhaps too enthusiastically, embrace the epidemic of change in our postindustrial society. Their view of "cultural lag" says that we have hardly given the human sciences a chance to help transform men and women so that they will continue to be human beings in this "brave new world."[5] All these views have something to contribute to the difficult task of coping with change. Yet our preoccupation with this aspect of accommodation to changing culture may divert us from the partnerships that might emerge in churches that put "safety last" and act out of a basic maladjustment with the present because of a longed-for future.

This maladjustment with the present is called *advent shock*.[6] Because of advent shock we seek to anticipate the future in what we do, opening ourselves to the working of God's Spirit and expecting the impossible. This provides an eschatological perspective for our discussion of the church and partnership. In such a perspective we will see ourselves as pilgrims on the way to tomorrow, searching out ways in which to express our freedom in Jesus Christ as a witnessing community.

ON THE WAY TO TOMORROW[7]

The church is on the way to the world of tomorrow because it already anticipates that world, living out of the memory of God's promised future. The forms of partnership that are the infrastructure of every community gathered in Christ's name partake of the constant tension of the *already—not yet.* The new focus of relationship in sharing a common history in Jesus Christ which sets us free for others has already happened in the events of God's saving and liberating action. Yet this new focus of relationship is in the process of continuing fulfillment, and on the way toward completion in the New World of God's tomorrow.[8]

As an eschatological community of exodus the church is on the move. Its work or mission is to be that part of the world which points to the promised intention of God for the whole world through actions that contradict the present in favor of peace, justice, freedom, and human dignity. The church is called to be the bearer of the image of future partnership *(koinōnia)* even as it carries out its mission of proclamation, celebration, and service. In so doing, it becomes a partner with God in the work of the Kingdom, as a "construction worker" and not just as an "interpreter" of God's future.[9]

Maladjustment with the Present

On its way to tomorrow the church suffers from advent shock or maladjustment with the present because of a longed-for future. When it longs, works, and prays for God's future of true humanity and shalom, the church finds itself a misfit in the *status quo.* For it is preoccupied with ways in which all oppressed persons, groupings, and nations can be brought into the human community as full participants and welcomed into partnership in service.

Maladjustment or advent shock means that the church is *infected with hope* in God's future in spite of the problems of the world in which it dwells. It longs with all of groaning creation for the revealing of "real live children of God," those who are set free to be partners with themselves, others, and God. With Paul, the church is infected with advent hope, expecting the unexpected, hoping against hope for God's liberation (Rom. 8:18–24; 4:18).

Maladjustment with the world is already an "assigned" part of the church's job description in postindustrial society, for it functions mainly in the private sector of society and is out of step with the public decision-making sectors of society. Such is the "feminization of the church" in American culture that clergy as a class are linked with women as a class in the popular mind.[10] Yet this too may be an advantage as we recognize the cultural bankruptcy of both the feudal *organic paradigm* and the industrial *mechanistic paradigm* for culture. If we are to find new forms of human personal and social interrelationships in the world of tomorrow, it is likely to be by turning toward what Gibson Winter calls a new *creative paradigm* of culture.[11] Such a paradigm would replace the hierarchy and domination of former social models with a model of creative interdependence. The church may be able to provide a liberated zone for the creative values to be nurtured and strengthened, turning what is now considered "vulnerability, weakness, helplessness" into new sources of strength.[12]

The church and its members may be maladjusted with the present, not only because they are hopeless optimists about God's promise and because they value humanistic and creative strengths, but also because they follow the life story of Jesus of Nazareth. Thus they are driven to look for Christ in the most *unlikely places:* among the poor and needy, with those who break with convention and seek out new life-styles, with the very persons whom the "real world" considers of no account. When this begins to happen it is likely that *koinōnia* might happen between many unlikely partners. Such a gift is described by Elizabeth O'Connor when she reflects on her experiences in the Church of the Saviour, Washington, D.C., and talks of the marks of the liberating community as commitment to: the poor; a life of dialogue; critical contemplation; reflection; and solitude.[13]

Such gifts also emerge among others who are no longer active in local parish churches because they have become so maladjusted with the present they also suffer *parish shock.* They have found themselves out of step with parishes that simply preserve the *status quo,* reinforcing the prejudices and injustices of our society by silence or active endorsement. In the United Church Board of Homeland Ministries, Susan Savell is a staff person working with Liberation Church Development, reaching out to church and community groups seeking to deepen and sustain their spiritual life in ministry. Each such group is different, yet each is committed in its own way to participate in God's liberating actions in and with the world.

> In New York City a group meets each Sunday night to worship, study the economic implications of the Gospel, and develop inclusive liturgical practices. In Boston's South End a multiracial team of ordained and lay ministers are working with neighborhood people for better housing, jobs, and resources for battered women and children. In San Francisco a group of Asian, White, Chicano, Black and Feminist church activists meet to plan ways of supporting each other's liberation work.[14]

Such a view of the church as an "enclave of the future," suffering from maladjustment with present society, clearly belongs to the model of church which Avery Dulles describes as the *servant church.*[15] In contrast to the other church models of *institution, mystical communion, sacrament,* and *herald,* the servant church is not in a privileged position in respect to the world, but rather seeks to participate in the work of God in the world, operating "on the frontier between the contemporary world and Christian tradition."[16] Its unity is found in the partnership of those who share in service to humanity, and its purpose is to share in God's Mission toward New Creation.

Dulles considers that the strength of such an understanding of the church, which has been popular since the 1960's, is its concern for communication between the church and the world, and its unwillingness to be turned in on itself.

> It seeks to give the Church a new relevance, a new vitality, a new modernity, and a new sense of mission. The effort on the Church's part to overcome its pride, its corporate egoism, and its callousness toward human misery promises to bring about a great spiritual renewal within the Church itself.[17]

Dulles claims, however, that the servant church model has no direct Biblical foundation, for ministry of service in the Gospels is a ministry of word and sacrament, rather than curative service. Furthermore, the servant is not "under orders" of the world but of God in working for others in humility. Ministry applies to all the offices of the church and is usually mutual ministry to one another and not toward the world. Dulles concludes that the foundation of the servant church model is found only indirectly in the image of the Suffering Servant used by Jesus to interpret his own ministry (Isa. 61:1; Luke 4:16–19).[18]

As Dulles points out in his book, no one church model is adequate in itself. Yet I would contend that the church that does not see a direct Biblical mandate to serve in the ministry and life-style of Jesus Christ has lost the heart of the story of God's service. Institution has a place as an expression of continuity and organization. Proclamation of the Word, Sacrament, and partnership in the body of Christ are all important aspects of the life of the church, but their purpose is for the building up of the body in the service of God's actions toward New Creation. In every age commitment to one who gave his life a ransom for all means that the church finds itself maladjusted with the present as it seeks to follow the life-style of one who himself was rejected by the religious leaders of his own time.

Biblical Images of Christian Community

Another way of looking at the servant model of the church on the way to tomorrow is to compare it directly with Biblical images of the church. Out of the ninety-six images of the church identified in his book *Images of the Church in the New Testament,* Paul Minear classifies four major clusters of analogies which dominated a broad sector of early Christian thought.[19] He points out that none of the images was church-centered. They all pointed beyond themselves to the realm in which God, Jesus Christ, and the Spirit were at work; to the mystery of God's plan for the fullness of time.[20] The community was free to use a riotous variety of metaphors because it saw itself as part of a dynamic process of the working of the Holy Spirit and looked to "the grace of the Lord Jesus Christ, the love of God, the communion [*koinōnia*] of the Holy Spirit" as its source of blessing (II Cor. 13:14).[21]

The four major clusters of analogies focus on images of the church as: the *people of God,* called by God to pilgrimage and covenant partnership; the *new humanity* as part of God's redemption of the world and new creation; a *fellowship of saints and slaves* who shared a life of interdependence; the *body of Christ,* sharing in his death and resurrection as members of his body, partners in his body and blood and in his ministry.[22]

It is interesting to note that all these clusters of meaning have been the source of our discussion of "Partnership with God." The image of the people of God was especially important to the description of *God's Arithmetic* and the stewardship of the covenant. The new humanity helped us to understand ourselves as *God's Utopia*, gifted by God as participants in New Creation. The fellowship of saints and slaves is an expression of *God's Self-Presentation* as Lord and Servant, and the invitation to share in a community of empowerment for service.

The body of Christ is a key metaphor for the understanding of *koinōnia as partnership* in Christ's life, death, and resurrection. As we saw in Chapter 1, Paul describes *koinōnia* (participation or partnership) in the cup of blessing and the broken bread as *koinōnia* in the blood and body of Christ (I Cor. 10:16–17). The body of Christ is frequently used by Paul to refer to the risen and glorified body of Christ with which believers are united by the power of the Holy Spirit and with which they will be fully united at the Parousia.[23] It is also used by Paul of the community of Christ's people or the church. Participation, or *koinōnia*, indicates that Christians have a share in Christ's body because in eating and drinking they express their community and unity together in the body of Christ as it is represented in the church, and they are united to Christ's heavenly body by the power of the Spirit.

From this brief discussion of the many configurations of metaphors and images of the church we can conclude that *diakonia* and *koinōnia* are not the only images available for describing what happens when two or three gather in the name of Christ. Yet they are important gifts to those who discover a way to share in serving God and others in the context of partnership in Jesus Christ.[24]

FREEDOM IN WITNESSING COMMUNITY

Just as the images of the church in the New Testament were constantly shifting as the Christian communities responded to the leading of the Lord in different contexts, the models and structures of church life have also changed over the centuries in response to particular needs. In searching for new models of

Christian community as the church moves toward the future, we know that these models and structures will continue to change. In each time and place the church is added on to the world of which it is a part, and a pluralistic world calls for a variety of images and structures. The expressions of Christian community or partnership in the church are living and dynamic relationships of persons that need to grow and change if they are to be responsible.

The key to this flexibility is the freedom of Jesus Christ. This freedom is sometimes very troubling because as Christians we do not know what to do with it.[25] Yet Paul reminds us that freedom is what the Christian life is all about, "For freedom Christ has set us free" (Gal. 5:1). The scandal of the cross is liberation from a rigidly defined style of life. Without the works of the law we are accepted as righteous through God's grace and set free to love our neighbor (Gal. 5).

This gift of freedom applies to all Christian communities of whatever type or confession, and it raises the question of whether the structures of our congregations are faithful to what the Spirit is saying to the churches. The trouble with freedom then is that we have to live out what that freedom means.[26] This is more difficult than following rules and regulations, and members of the Christian community find themselves responsible for their own exercise of freedom with others and for others. Perhaps some of the things we have learned about partnership will shed some light on the way freedom can be exercised responsibly in the context of a witnessing community.

Pluralistic Structures

In a pluralistic world the social forms or structures of Christian community will take on many shapes as they seek to embody an understanding of partnership as a solidarity of service. Social pluralism is the result of a process of social differentiation initiated by industrial development that results in a variety of "worlds" corresponding to economic needs. Arend van Leeuwen has indicated three essential features of the pluralistic society: (1) No one ideology dominates completely, or the society will become totalitarian. (2) There is acceptance of diversity not in the sense of "relativism" but in the sense of a number of different options for one's world view, beliefs, and actions. (3)

Society has a dynamic nature in which new groups emerge and work upon one another and are drawn into the process of change.[27]

In response to these various sectors or "worlds," churches need to have a strong self-identity about the meaning and purpose of their own calling by God which can be shared with others. For Christians, "something really matters," and that something is that God's love be known in and through every type of social culture or subculture. In order to share this message, churches need to be diversified in their programs and resources of people, funds, time, and property so that they are added on to all the "worlds," and not just to the private sector or the nuclear family.

A good example of this need for diversity of program and structure can be seen in the listing of types of alternative family structures in Chapter 4. Some of these are frequently neglected by the parish type of churches. In particular, we might mention the lack of conscious and affirmative ministry to single persons; to handicapped persons; and to those excluded from church life because of racism, classism, sexism, and heterosexism.[28]

One congregation that has developed an "instinct for greater inclusiveness" in its ministry to urban residents is Good Shepherd Faith Church. One of its members, Jim Comer, responded to the call issued by the pastor, Dick Symes, to testify at the Philadelphia hearings of the United Presbyterian Church Task Force on Homosexuality. Jim began by saying: "First of all, I must tell you that up to this moment I have never referred to myself as an 'avowed' homosexual. But starting now, that's what I am." A former schoolteacher turned actor and writer, Jim considered himself abnormal in New York City only in that he still went to church. In describing the ministry of this church, he said:

> There's good reason why I sometimes get myself up on Sunday morning. I have worshipped for almost eight years in a very special congregation . . . which has been a real family to me. I've gotten to know a great variety of loving people. I've sung solos, read Scriptures, taken care of the nursery, entertained at church dinners, written articles for the newsletter, and been a full and grateful participant in the life of the church. I have experienced a sense of community—of concern

and love, respect and tolerance, which has made me want to stay a part of the church.[29]

There is also a great need for diversity of structures in conjunction with the relation of the church to society. Over the years the church has played a variety of roles in Western society. In medieval society it was a "nonvariable" serving the function of public cult. In modern society the church became a "dependent variable" as part of the private sector which provided comfort and support for the *status quo.* In postmodern society its role should not only reflect earlier stages of development but also become one of an "independent variable," not trying to call the shots for the society as in the Middle Ages, nor being told what to do in society as in modern times, but joining with those who are intent for change toward human liberation to make an independent witness to the promise of God's New Creation in every social structure and every part of the globe.[30] As in all ages the social structures of the church will reflect the way human beings organize their lives in the structures of organization. In this sense they should *fit,* or be incarnated into those structures. Yet in all ages there also need to be *misfit* structures where these are needed to make an independent critique of the *status quo.*

One emerging structure of our period is that of the *movement,* or wide variety of collective attempts to bring about social change. There is no one organizational structure in such loosely connected groups, but they share a common goal. Often, as with the peace movement, the civil rights movement, and the women's movement, the common purpose was that of contradicting the injustice and inhumanity of society and of the churches who supported this *status quo.* Within the larger movements are many Christian groups both following and taking initiative at different times. Conservative movements of the right have the same nature, although they have a different ideological thrust or agenda.

A second structure that obviously emerges in contemporary society is the *system,* or complex of interlocking institutions. As society itself becomes a complex of systems the church finds itself drawn into its own multinational and national coalitions that seek to develop means for dealing with systems. Some of these have grown out of ecumenical movements and have led to

federations, consolidations, consortiums, or ecumenical organizations. The problem with such consolidation in the churches
is that in adapting to the pattern of systemic social control they
may sell out to the power structures of society which are able
to provide economic support. They also find little support at the
grass-roots level where persons look to their churches to provide
humanizing and supportive structures in the face of impersonal
systems.

A third structure that continues to be popular in a pluralistic
society is the *ad hoc group,* or voluntary grouping that meets to
accomplish a specific and usually limited purpose. Such groups
take on a wide variety of forms both within and outside established church structures and can be found as part of a movement
or a system, or completely independent of other church institutions. As the church finds itself in diaspora situations where it
is a tiny minority, such "missionary structures" may become an
important part of the witness of larger church institutions.[31]

An example of this ad hoc grouping in the name of Christ is
Shalom, Inc., in East Harlem. For eight years it consisted of a
group of people drawn from East Harlem, as well as from other
parts of New York City and of the nation, who wanted to be in
the "business of shalom," working with adults, youth, and children to create bridges between the artistic world of New York
and the youth of East Harlem through intercultural dramatic
and musical programs. The program was facilitated by Harold
Eads, a man with amazing gifts for bringing persons together
across racial, economic, and geographical barriers so that they
could minister to one another bringing wholeness to one another's lives.

In order to continue this program, Eads had to raise the
money through its richer supporters and to carry out a tentmaking ministry through teaching in an experimental school. Members of a team ministry each contributed skills part time while
supporting themselves by other means, yet they brought signs
of hope and joy to many young people caught in a ghetto of
poverty. The ministry of Harold Eads was one of availability to
all without regard to their religious background or life-style. In
fact, his willingness to share city life at all hours of the day or
night with those in need brought his life to a sudden end when
he was knifed to death by someone who had taken advantage

of his hospitality. Shalom is not always peace. Sometimes as the hymn says, it is "strife closed in the sod."[32] But that gift of life and cohumanity does happen among persons and it grows in spite of the cost, in ad hoc groups the world over.

The World Council of Churches' study of the Missionary Structure of the Congregation led to many suggestions for ways in which the church could reorient its thinking toward the needs and the agenda of the world. A variety of church structures were suggested such as: *family structures* whose locus was residential and whose function was the service of a particular segment of God's world in which it was located, so that a family or community of faith emerged; *permanent availability* structures oriented toward long-term tasks of making services available to persons without any "strings attached"; *task force structures* formed around a particular need or function and of shorter duration.[33] Contrary to Avery Dulles, those who worked on these forms of servant church did not think that the world decided how service should be rendered. They believed that "God sets the agenda" but that God's agenda has to do with a mission of service in the world.[34]

Now, some ten years later, one wonders why these suggestions have had so little effect on the life of the church as a whole. One reason was that the church continued to think of the parish structure as normative and the other structures as experiments. Therefore, when the funding and the liberal optimism disappeared the "so-called" experiments died for lack of institutionalized form. Many of the radical leaders of such church renewal were co-opted by the national church bureaucracy and then, in turn, laid off when the church structures were reorganized and regionalized. At the same time the emergence of the self-identity of black and other Third World groups led to emphasis on self-liberation by means that were indigenous to the constituencies involved.

Many other factors could be cited, including the conservative trend of the nation and of religious groups. Yet there are some underlying thought patterns involved here that need to be pointed out. Church-centered thinking about the role of the church has continued to lead churches to think of themselves as central to God's concern with a primary duty to make converts rather than as instruments of God's Mission to the world.

Morphological fundamentalism, or belief that church structures or organizations are divinely ordained and unchangeable, continues to undercut proposals for pluralistic structures. Those who want renewal generally fear too much change or liberation, and those who search for liberation often move out and create their own and ad hoc structures. The clerical structures of the church continue to make it impossible to empower the whole people of God to carry out a wide variety of ministries in the world with or without theological education and certification. There is still not an adequate educational base at the grass roots that makes it possible for large numbers of persons to catch the vision of a servant church.

In such a situation new attention must be focused on the way in which partnership may arise in a variety of situations to overcome the barriers between church and world, clergy and laity, educated and unschooled. For in our time there is no less need for growing communities of nurture and service. As O'Connor points out:

> No single relationship, no matter how cherished, is adequate for the nurturing of a person. Therefore, communities of caring and thus of hope must be built in a despairing age. For this to happen the churches must consider the matter of their own transformation, so that their structures do not contradict their revolutionary gospel or prevent the "acting out" of that gospel in small faith communities.[35]

Christian Life-Style

The question of what pluralistic structure, when or where, becomes one of stewardship as we seek to follow the life-style of Jesus Christ. We discover the points of our own involvement at any one period of time in the light of our talents, faith, opportunity to serve, and what seems to be the calling of God. Responsible membership in the life of the church means having the courage and faith to choose when, where, and how God has called us to serve, with the help of the Christian community and its faith, and then having the courage and faith to pay the cost.

Christian style is the way in which Christ forms and shapes the lives of women and men. Because it is the power of Christ which shapes us, we can speak of Christian *style*. Yet this style is always expressed in many *styles* which result from human cultural and historical particularity. The number of different life-styles that can result from life in a pluriform society makes it very difficult to identify the nature of Christian style in a modern world. In other ages it was possible to identify the more or less static roles of peasant, or monk, or nobility and to express the meaning of the Christian life-style according to these models.[36]

Today, however, Christian life-style has to be flexible and changing as are the models and callings of contemporary life. Style becomes authentic in the eyes of the world, not because of its particular characteristics, but because one's actions are perceived as consistent with one's expressed values and beliefs. What makes a style of life Christian is the way it mirrors the commitment of a person to Jesus Christ and to his promise of new freedom in service.

This life by promise is precarious because it is life lived by hope as well as faith. There is no one set of religious customs that will afford assurance that it is in fact a Christian life-style. Yet life by God's promise does have certain Christological perspectives that give it a Christian style. The first is a perspective of *freedom for the future.* The Christian stands with Paul in solidarity with the groaning world, yet with a hope in God's future that makes possible actions that anticipate God's promised future (Rom. 8:18–25). The second perspective is that of *freedom for others.* Because of a desire to live Jesus' life-style of service the Christian becomes not simply "other directed" but "Christ directed." As the love of Christ continues to shape the Christian's life, he or she gains a perspective of freedom for others which is expressed in solidarity and availability to those whose lives are shared. The last perspective is that of *freedom for the gospel.* In joining God's Mission of New Creation and inviting others to take part, the Christian is able to celebrate the good news of Christ's victory now, living as much as possible in the anticipation of the completion of the New Age.

As we look at some of the perspectives of freedom that are part of Christian life-style, we see much that points us to the discussion of the meaning of partnership. For indeed, style is another way of describing what happens when there is a new focus of relationship among persons in Jesus Christ which sets them free for others. There is never any one blueprint, but, nevertheless, style emerges out of a common commitment to others involving responsibility, vulnerability, trust, and a sharing of gifts. It grows through a common struggle to live out the gospel by moving toward the service of God and others in concrete contexts of human physical and spiritual need. Above all, such style is always ready to be surprised at the gifts and challenges of God, looking expectantly with others for *more to come!*

THE CHURCH AND PARTNERSHIP

In church tradition theologians have sought to describe the essential ingredients of church life in a variety of ways. The Reformers indicated where the true church was to be found by speaking of the *marks* as Word properly preached and the Sacraments properly administered, but they mentioned other marks as well.[37] Roman Catholic and Protestant alike agreed on the *signs* as an indication of the presence of the church through unity, holiness, catholicity, and apostolicity. And both groups also went on to give other *descriptions* of the church. Today when we are not as focused on identifying one particular form of church over against another, we can be more concerned about the way in which the church manifests its function by sharing in the mission of Christ. Where this partnership takes place there is a new focus of relationship that sets us free for service.

In such a setting the marks of the church cease to be a way of trying to establish the true church by identifying its boundaries, and they become indications of the presence of Christ at the center of a community open to the world. The presence of Christ is to be discovered not only by such indications as those listed above, or even only through the gifts of *kērygma, koinōnia, diakonia,* and *leitourgia* (Acts 2:41–47). The presence is also to be discovered when gifts of serendipity, synergy, and sharing happen in the life and mission of the church. As partnership with Christ grows among us we discover unexpected ways God leads us in new directions or provides us with new hope in the midst of despair. In partnership the number of gifts seems to multiply, so that two becomes three or much more as we search out ways to share the love of God with others. Out of the transformation of common reality the love of Christ shapes the church as an instrument of God's purpose so that its members may share as partners in God's New Creation (Acts 4:32–37).

Eschatological Perspectives

Partnership is crucial to both the form and the function of the church, because it is out of *koinōnia* that hope is born and activated. As Dom Helder Camâra has said, using a Brazilian proverb:

> When we dream alone it is only a dream. But when we dream together it is the beginning of reality.[38]

In partnership we dream and work together for justice and peace and for the establishment of God's rule on earth. Yet we know two things about our actions and prayers. One is that the church is not simply identified with the Kingdom of God and the other is that it is not simply identified with *koinōnia*. The church points to the Kingdom and is a prolepsis or anticipation of the New Age, made possible by the presence of the Holy Spirit. Yet the Kingdom for which the church works and prays is God's and it will come in God's own time as a gracious gift. This is a source of great hope, for it is not all up to the church! In the same way *koinōnia* is a gift of God's Spirit through the promised presence of Christ among those gathered in his name. It is not an ecclesiastical possession that can be restricted to any one group of people.

If we look to the Bible to see how it is that Christ promised to be with us, we are perhaps somewhat surprised to find that promise clearly applied not only to those who gather in Christ's name or break bread in his name but also to the poor. In Matthew 25 we have an eschatological interpretation of history that leads us to suspect that the true church is present "in the mission of the believers *and* [as Moltmann points out] the suffering of the least of these."[39]

Let us turn to listen more closely to Matt. 25:31–46 following Hans Hoekendijk's interpretation of this eschatological parable.[40] Throughout history the church has listened to this parable with the understanding smile of self-recognition. It was delighted to find its own Magna Carta, its own overall service program at last confirmed by the King on the throne, before all the nations. Sometimes the church has been bold enough to suggest that the Son of Man was not quite up-to-date, and has added to the list of those in need. Others have suggested that this is a story about the final act of church history, ignoring the fact that it is not the church which is gathered at the judgment seat but people of all nations who will be received in audience.

Perhaps it could be said that this is a parable of the last act in history; not of the church but of humankind. In a sense it is, but even this may not be the real focus of the text. Hoekendijk suggests that we find here the *history of Jesus, told by himself* in a definitive fashion. What does Jesus say here about his own history? The story seems to say that the Parousia, the coming of Christ, takes place whenever a person recognizes and affirms the claim to his love that goes out from another person in need. That's Parousia, *advent,* the coming of Christ! He is as much present in the poor as he is present in the act of breaking the bread and pouring the wine, and the two belong together. This is perhaps what distinguishes the church from all other religious groupings. It celebrates the presence of its Lord in a twofold way: in the Eucharist and among the poor in the shape of humanity. In reaching out the cup of cold water we reach out to the one who desires to share his life story with us; a story full of that strange eschatological arithmetic of the Kingdom.

Eschatological hermeneutics leads us to ask the question: How can the church manifest *koinōnia* in its midst? In the light of tradition we find the church rather sure that Christ is present in acts of charity, but in the experience of the poor and the oppressed there are many questions about whether indeed the church has been or is "partner." An eschatological clue in this matter comes from the understanding of Christ's risen and glorified body to which the servers and the served are joined in a solidarity of partnership. In trying to live this out we discover anew a source of advent shock, for a church in poverty would be so maladjusted with the present that it would even be led to make coalitions with "fringe" groups of the left in order to bring about some humanizing changes.[41] Next we are led to ask: How is it that the church can manifest authentic forms of partnership in which the gospel is preached as good news for the poor (Luke 4:18)?

God's Self-Presentation

The clues for partnership from God's self-presentation may be of help in discussing the relationship of the church and its calling to God's Mission. The two clues that are of particular relevance are: (1) the context of partnership is not subordination but service; (2) service performed in partnership calls for a form of calculated inefficiency that allows room for all partners to grow and participate fully.

In the New Testament, Christian calling and gifts of the Spirit are inseparable from service according to Käsemann:

> There is no divine gift which does not bring with it a task. There is no grace which does not move to action. Service is not merely the consequence but the outward form of the realization of grace.[42]

One way of discussing how we might carry out this mandate of *diakonia* is to examine the various forms it might take. These forms include *curative diakonia*, healing and helping victims of society; *preventive diakonia*, attempting to curtail the development of social ills that victimizes human life; and *prospective diakonia*, attempting to open the situation for free actualization of human life.[43] The kind of *diakonia* that we would want for our own life is the last kind. We would not want to be helped after we were crushed, if we could have had justice that would have eliminated the destructive social structures beforehand. Yet, in fact, there is place for all three and all three types reflect Biblical motifs.

We can see curative *diakonia* in stories like that of the good Samaritan in which the response is simply one of helping the neighbor in need (not changing the police or ambulance service). Preventive *diakonia* can be seen in the attempt to evolve traditions and laws to fit the changing patterns of life in Israel. For instance, Deuteronomy rewrites the law, placing it in a sermon context and liberalizing the laws to reflect the impact of prophetic tradition. Women and orphans are protected and sanctuaries are provided for those who have committed murder and seek a fair trial. Prospective *diakonia* is seen not only in the eschatological passages of the vision of New Creation as in Romans 8 but also in the parables. In God's rule, in the New Age, things are ordered in a different way: talents multiply, lost sheep are found, the poor are fed, and prodigals are welcomed.

Today such a typology of ministry might be worked out in relation to any form of *diakonia:* world hunger, world peace, federal harassment of movement groups, ecology and nuclear threat, multinational corporations, and all the rest. One of the first persons to work out this typology of types of *diakonia* did so by reflecting on his own work for the liberation of handicapped persons in the Netherlands.[44] In his action-reflection he discovered that there were not only distinct ministries involved but also distinct actions and constituencies.

Curative *diakonia* involved working with the handicapped to obtain medical service, social counseling programs, and raising money from those ready to give to such needs. Preventive *diakonia* involved changing the situation itself so that disabilities that caused problems were removed: getting ramps built, better housing, training for jobs. This involved working with businessmen, contractors, government regulators. Prospective *diakonia* became a nationwide project, including radio appeals, interpretation, governmental support to build a whole new town in which handicapped people could live together with others in a town designed to meet their needs so that as much as possible they could live as others. It involved the conviction of a group of people that this impossibility was possible.

One key factor for all types of *diakonia* is the participation of those who are the ones being served in the actual planning and mutual serving of others. Without this element of partnership in service all the forms of service remain "Band-Aids" which perpetuate the problems of those "being served." The understanding of the church as a place where persons become *mutual* partners and *subjects* of the efforts for change has much to say for those who see the life story of Jesus as one of solidarity with suffering humanity.

Calculated inefficiency is very important here. For it is just at the point where those seeking to be true partners let their brothers and sisters have sufficient space to design and carry out their own projects of self-identity and empowerment that true mutual *diakonia* comes alive. God has chosen to become weak with us in a calculated inefficiency that makes it possible that even the church may be an instrument of God's work.[45] God consistently chooses those who are of no account to do ministry so that no one can boast (I Cor. 1:26–31). It is this style of God's own self-presentation which helps us to remember that it is we who are served by God out of love, and to seek out the ways in which we might become God's servant church. Meanwhile we ask ourselves with Hoekendijk:

Does the church by any chance exist for any other purpose than for this *diakonia* to the world? Can it after all experience a *koinōnia*, e.g., in the fellowship of the World Church, which is not identical with a participation *(koinōnia)* in Christ's apostolic ministry? And is there another way of partaking in the Gospel than as partners in the furtherance of the Gospel? (Phil. 1:5).[46]

6

FLIGHT FROM MINISTRY

One of the continuing symptoms of future shock in the church is the crisis of confidence in the forms of Christian ministry. All our attempts at renewal of the church and the development of new forms of mission and ministry for laity and clergy have not alleviated the problems that we feel in our bones and hear expressed in seminaries and churches. Questions rise in our minds about whether an ordained "clerical caste" is the most faithful way to express partnership of the people of God in the New Age. At the moment, when women are moving into clerical professions in increasing numbers, many are beginning to ask whether or not ordination as we know it ought to continue in the church.

In looking at vocation as God's call to freedom and ministry or service, we can see that some of our problems are derived from the ecclesial and social contradictions that have arisen over the use of the words "vocation" and "ministry" in the practice of church and society. Vocation *(klēsis),* or God's call to freedom in a witnessing community, has become confused with work, profession, or religious order and has lost its close connection with the witnessing community *(koinōnia)* as its context. Ministry *(diakonia),* or service in the New Age, has become confused with clerical profession and has lost its close connection with God's free gifts *(charismata)* that belong to all the people of God. Sometimes we look around and wonder, Whatever happened to the priesthood of *all* believers?

Of course, problems over ministry and vocation are by no means recent phenomena. An early manual on ministry from the fourth century, written by Gregory of Nazianzus, is called

"About Flight."[1] The continual situation of ministry for anyone called by God in any age is risky. As Gregory warns, freely chosen *diakonia* in any generation is a difficult and almost impossible life-style that leads to the temptation of pride. Martin Luther's advice to men seeking to be pastors contains warnings about this difficulty.

> Therefore my advice is: Flee, all ye that would live in safety; begone, young men, and do not enter upon this holy estate, unless you are determined to preach the Gospel, and are able to believe that you are not one whit better than the laity.[2]

In our generation the tendency toward flight from the temptations of professional ministry is even more justified, in the light of the present situation of clerical ministry with its institutional captivity and oppressive forms.

The whys and wherefores of this malaise in ministry have been documented over and over.[3] Yet we are still at the beginning of finding a theological consensus on the meaning of ministry that can be translated into new partnerships for mission that move beyond the divisions of race, sex, class, and sexual orientation.[4] Perhaps we can make one small contribution to this search for partnership in service if we try to look at some of the pride, failure, confusion, discrimination, and mystification that seem to cloud the meaning of vocation and ministry for the people of God. We will look at the call to service in a New Age, then at the relationship of clergy and laity, before discussing ministry and partnership.

CALL TO SERVICE IN A NEW AGE

God's call to freedom and service in a New Age is experienced today in our lives in many ways. These experiences are interpreted through the accumulated meanings of "calling" and "ministry" in the traditions of church and culture. The meaning of service was discussed in the light of God's self-presentation as Servant and Lord in Chapter 3. Here we need to focus on God's call to partnership in that service, and what that call means for people struggling with the meaning of their own vocation and ministry.

God's Call to Freedom

When asked to describe the meaning of vocation, laypersons, pastors, students, and teachers seem more likely to describe their *response to God's call,* speaking about how they see or do it rather than the why or how of God's call. This inductive approach is not surprising, for we do theology as a response to God's action in reaching out to us and it often makes more sense to talk about that experience than about a particular doctrinal description of God's call.

Some of the descriptions people give in response to the question, What is vocation and what does it mean in your life? are in the area of the *orientation* that such a call gives to one's life. Some people stress vocation as a calling into a relationship of faith and commitment with God that is expressed in whatever they do, and not in any one particular task or life-style. Others speak of vocation as a style of service for others in response to God's call. Still others stress their attitudes or values that are shaped as a response to a God who cares. Thus they are called to be listening, discerning, and caring people with others.

Another group of persons focus their answers to the question of vocation on the area of *religious call* from God. They might single out a religious vocation or priesthood as descriptive of their vocation. Or they might describe a call to ministry in which they are struggling to find the way to respond in terms of concrete life decisions, such as: whether or not to be ordained, or whether to work in the church or in another sector of society.

A third group of persons respond primarily to the secular connotation of vocation as *work or profession.* In describing call in this way, they look upon vocation as what one does for pay, prestige, or survival, depending on one's class or situation. Vocation is usually contrasted here with avocation as unpaid activity. Along with the other descriptions, these responses reflect the various understandings of vocation found in the Bible and in historical development. It is important, therefore, to look at the evolution of the ways God's call came to be understood.

Vocation in the Light of Tradition

Vocation understood in Biblical perspective finds its basis in *Tradition* as the dynamic and continuing process of God's "handing over of Jesus Christ into the hands of all generations and nations.'"[5] In the Biblical view, Tradition is not a static deposit *(parathēkē)*, as described in Jude 3 and I Tim. 6:20, but a dynamic action of relationship, or handing over *(paradosis)*, as described in Matt. 17:22 and Rom. 8:31–33. We need to see there that vocation is related directly to this sending action of God. Vocation is in fact the experience of God's Traditioning action in our lives. Both vocation and Tradition are used most abundantly in the New Testament in their verbal or active forms.[6]

The English word *voc-ation* is related to the Latin word for voice *(vox)*. It refers to God's voice or call by which God calls things into being. "And God said, 'Let there be light'; and there was light" (Gen. 1:3). God calls things into being and then addresses them to become what God plans them to be.[7]

In the Old Testament, *qara'* (to make oneself heard) and *shalach* (to be sent on a general or specific task) are root expressions of call. To hear the voice is to be sent to accomplish a job. Election is calling to service as the people of God. The voice of God is the beginning of one's calling. Thus Isa. 41:9 declares to Israel:

> You whom I took from the ends of the earth,
>   and called from its farthest corners,
> saying to you, "You are my servant,
>   I have chosen you and not cast you off."

In the New Testament, vocation and calling go together. God's call has its effect in vocation to participate in what God has planned for all humankind. A later text, "God our Savior, who desires all [people] to be saved and to come to the knowledge of the truth" (I Tim. 2:3–4), expresses one perspective on the job description of all those who have responded to the call of God. Paul's earlier text in I Cor. 7:20 indicates the same "job description": to live out the Christ event in our lives. But this later text raises a further question of what Paul means by saying that we are to live it out in the place, state, or condition in which we were called.

Our various understandings of vocation have been affected by the wide variety of *religious and cultural traditions* that have grown up around the concept of call or calling. These traditions are an important part of our own identity and that of our confessional group, but they are not of ultimate significance in relation to how we might want to live out our faith. While vocation in the New Testament referred to the general calling of Christ, the emphasis was shifted in monastic tradition and Roman Catholic tradition, so that the word was reserved for those who had a religious calling. Those with a vocation were the ones who had left the world and the profane things of life to follow a higher and sacred calling. Thus, even today, Roman Catholic children are often asked if they have "A Vocation," as a priest, sister, or brother in a religious order.

Luther, who coined the word *Beruf* as a word referring both to vocation (call) and to station (condition and occupation in life), fought the established view of the Roman Catholic Church.[8] In Luther's view, all persons are called by God, but only in the place they are, which is to be the context of service and love. John Calvin had a similar view, but stressed the importance of living out one's calling in whatever job one had as a means of giving glory to God. This view that one's secular job was a means of serving God is sometimes called worldly asceticism.

In the secularization process of Western society, what is still called the Protestant work ethic has been translated into white, male, middle-class values. Work and station in life are no longer related to the calling of God but only to identity and self-worth. At the same time, the distinction between religious and secular vocation in the Roman Catholic tradition has also largely been retained, with vocation becoming a specialized word referring to profession, and, in the case of the church, to a religious or clerical occupation.

The human *traditioning process* in which the still living and evolving past calls for commitment in shaping human community in the present and future includes all these confessional and social traditions and much more.[9] They are functioning unconsciously or consciously to shape our future. As we struggle with what our own response to God's call might be at any given time, it is helpful to be aware of the changes in the meaning of vocation. The Christian concept of vocation may be a living and evolving past for us as we come to see it more clearly as God's call to freedom in community. It can become a central means of shaping our lives as we open our hearts to receive our vocation new each day and to discover what it means to be God's servant and to live this out.

In looking at vocation in relation to the various types of tradition, we must emphasize that calling is not just something that applies to those who are seeking clerical ordination or religious vocation. Nor does it mean that we must exercise our call within the church, although it is very much related to communal nurture and support as its context. Calling does not always mean that we have one "station," in Luther's understanding of the term, but it does mean that we should begin where we are to act our way into the many things we may do and places we may find to participate in God's work of creating a more human society.

CLERGY AND LAITY

If there is only one call of God in Jesus Christ extended to all persons, those who respond to the call all become ministers or servants whether they are functioning as laity or as clergy. If there is One Call and One Ministry, then partnership between laity and clergy is crucial for the life and mission of the church. Yet it is at this point that partnership often breaks down. In order to analyze the barriers that have grown up between the two groups more clearly, let us look at the nature of systemic oppression as it applies to the clergy and the laity as oppressors and oppressed; and then at changing roles in ministry.

Oppressors and Oppressed

In our discussion and thoughts there is usually a certain reluctance to identify ourselves with either oppressed or oppressor groups. Many of us do not like the language. It is too harsh and seems to apply only in situations of extreme deprivation or repression. Others prefer other terms for what they consider to be an overused cliché. They would like to speak of limitations, social evil, sin, lack of choice. Yet this reluctance probably stems from the difficult emotions that underlie the words and a lack of understanding of what is meant.

In this regard it is important to distinguish between *deliberate oppression,* which arises out of deliberate and individual actions, and *systemic oppression,* which arises from interaction of various elements comprising a social system. Systemic oppression may exist without there being any conscious oppressive actions against others, and it is only by looking at the social systems themselves that we see the interaction of variables that can be modified to change the oppressive way in which a system operates. The elimination of oppression requires not just reform and change in individual persons, but new rules for society so that the system of society is less oppressive. This can be seen in a very elementary way in the game of Monopoly. The goal of the game is for people to lose and win, and the rules help this to happen as the "rich get richer." If the goal of Monopoly were for everyone to stay in the game as long as possible, then the rules of the game would have to change so that there was an equalization of profit.[10]

Oppression comes in many forms (physical, psychological, social, political, ecclesial). When we meet it among ourselves and in our world it often brings pain and guilt. Some of us ignore the systemic nature of racism, sexism, heterosexism, or classism. We say: "I'm not part of that mess. I don't hurt people!" Or we try to stay at a distance saying, "That's what happens somewhere out there in the world, but not to me in my home or in my church!" Yet in the church, distinctions of race, gender, sexual orientation, and class often receive reinforcement and are maintained with "God's blessing." The sort of divisions that have prevented partnership between laity and clergy are part of this "conspiracy" to divide the people of God.[11]

Recently, when I was speaking on the meaning of liberation and mission one man said, "Ministers are the most oppressed people around, don't you think?" I found myself answering, "Well, they are both oppressed and oppressors, because *all* of us participate in the forms of oppression that are part of the structures of church life, clergy and laity alike."

Clergy are oppressors of laity for many reasons. They participate in the hierarchical structures of church organization that give them power over laity. Along with their position, their training and status as an ordained person virtually assure that, normally, they have the last word. Whatever their style may be, it will be likely to become the style of the parish served until a new pastor and style come along.[12] The clergy have been "set apart" and therefore are somehow more holy, more religious than others even in denominations that say ordination is only functional and does not change status. Clergy can and do guard this status because of their privileges regarding preaching and Sacraments. Sometimes people from oppressed groups buy into this "status thing" more than others as a compensation and means of moving out of their subordinate roles.

The laity are largely "second-class Christians" in comparison, because they are often nonprofessionals, and unpaid (being paid is an important indicator of identity and worth in our society and the church). They are often less educated theologically and less articulate in theological language. Therefore they are largely cast in a role of domesticated service for the clergy as unpaid assistants. The churches' forms of organization seem to promote a form of collusion between clergy and laity. The clergy need the laity to be dependent in order to bolster up their authority and the laity need an authority figure who can be their "professional Christian."

Yet *clergy are also oppressed.* They suffer an identity crisis, cut off from viable role models for their work in a modern society of specialists, and frequently unsure what they or the church should do. They are generalists in an age of specialists who seem to do counseling, administration, community organization, education, far better than they. There is a wide discrepancy between their education and calling to service and much of what they do.[13]

Because clergy continue to minister mainly in local parishes, they find themselves working in the private sector, cut off from other parts of the working world, and isolated with other subordinated groups such as women and children. They are dependent on the church for a salary to support their families and in danger of loss of salary or position because of the displeasure of parishioners of the church or of the bureaucracy. Women clergy who are feminists are likely to run into the disapproval of church members if they combine their parish work with advocacy for women or begin working for nonsexist liturgy and language. Women and men who are social activists for any cause will also run into this tension.

Clergy also are sometimes isolated and may have difficulty relating to others in their own profession. They must relate to laity with care not to be overfamiliar with certain ones, and they have been taught to view other ministers as competitors with whom they often engage in horizontal violence and superego trips to bolster up the fragility of their roles. Women clergy are even more isolated because of the threat they pose to their male peers and their exclusion from the informal male network.

The point of illustrating some of the ways the system of ordination in churches leads to oppression of both clergy and laity is not to say that no one is fulfilled in his or her ministry and calling, but rather to say that there are many structural aspects of the system that lead to a breakdown of partnership in congregations and denominations. Not only does this produce lack of trust and joy in the common witness and service, but also it tends to conceal God's call to service in a New Age, and the wide variety of roles that might be included in the ministry and mission of the church. Yet there are signs that some of the roles of ministry are changing, and perhaps these may in turn help to adjust the system as we know it toward greater partnership and flexibility.

Changing Roles in Ministry

Theological and Biblical research has helped to clarify our views of ministry in relation to vocation, and our analysis of the system may have helped us to see some of its problems. Perhaps we can find some clues for alternative roles by looking at ways people are working themselves into new forms of partnership and new thinking about ministry. These changing roles point us toward a future where those serving in Christ's name (whether paid or volunteer, ordained or not) will probably carry out their work in a variety of different fashions. Some of these roles have been around for a long while, and others are just beginning to emerge. In order to illustrate possible changes in role, let us look at things that are beginning to happen.

Remembering a tradition that goes back to Paul's *self-supporting ministry* as a tentmaker, women and men are moving into tentmaking or self-supporting ministries (Acts 18:3). With the decline in financial resources and memberships, and with such a great variety of tasks to be undertaken in this country and abroad, many people find that they have to support themselves by other work in addition to their regular ministry. This may not be as difficult in the future, if the possibilities for a four-day

or three-day workweek become a reality. Couples and community groups are increasingly searching for ways to share part-
time work and part-time child care, study, or volunteer work.
It may be that our vocations will increasingly be not necessarily
what we are paid for, but what we choose to do that brings
meaning to our lives.[14] An example of this attitude toward vocation may be seen in the fact that almost twice as many people
serve overseas as volunteers than are paid by the Program
Agency of The United Presbyterian Church U.S.A.[15]

With an increasing number of women entering the ordained
ministry there is a growing pattern of *clergy couples,* both of
whom are recognized by their respective denominations as having ministerial standing as clergy.[16] Sometimes these couples
work as a team in one church, either on one salary or on two
salaries. Sometimes they take different jobs located within com-
muting distance. The problems such couples face are not too
different from those of other working couples in relation to child
care, coordination of schedules, finding two jobs in the same
vicinity. However, they have two additional problems related to
sexism in the churches. A woman is still expected to play a
stereotyped role as pastor's wife, and there is reluctance to
recognize her as a pastor in her own right and to pay her an
equal salary. The other is that the couple are working to find a
new life-style for their marriage and their ministries at the same
time. Thus they must work doubly hard to overcome cultural
stereotypes about their masculine and feminine roles without
many role models and often with little support from denominations and churches.[17]

Even as society changes at an increasing rate, there are
changes beginning to take place in the length of any particular
form of ministry. Although denominational structures and pen-
sion systems work to discourage such a procedure, an increasing
number of people will be set apart for *special ministries of shorter
duration.* Even if the intention is that of longer duration when
the call is approved, it often can lead to new changes as personal
interests or the needs of a community shift. The projection for
the United States is that the average worker will change careers
three to five times in a lifetime and will need continuing education. This could also happen in the church if it got over some
of its "clerisy" hang-ups that assume that lifelong clerical ordi-

nation is the only faithful way to order church life.[18]

Where the mission of the church to the world is the focus of a particular gathered community it is likely that paid ministry will not be as dependent on ordination or as limited to sacramental functions as is presently the case. Rather, the person paid might be the person who needs to be paid, or the person who has particular expertise that can help a congregation in its ministry. For instance, a church involved in mission in the political sphere or in the area of ministry to the aging might pay experts in those fields for a limited period of time while having those who preach and administer the Sacraments work as volunteers.[19]

In spite of the resistance by the churches and the new programs such as that of the Association of Theological Schools in the United States and Canada to help train clergy who will fit the existing *status quo* in the churches, theological education begins to follow a *variety of models.*[20] These seek to liberate students to gain a theological education, while at the same time providing opportunity for exploring a professional skill such as teaching, social work, or law. Education in many places will be related to actual life experience and be a continuing process while people are working. Already many women and men find this more realistic for their needs. Women and Third World groups are especially interested in ways of pursuing theological education while continuing their ministries at home, in the church, and in society.[21]

If some of these changes begin to spread, clergy may no longer be viewed as "professional Christians" who have all the gifts of the Spirit by virtue of ordination. With so many people working in paid and volunteer ministries, the churches may very well appoint different people to do the different jobs now left to the clergy, such as administration, worship, social action, nurture, counseling, calling, theological reflection. Such a style of *corporate pastorate* is already in existence in some chaplaincy teams and some churches, such as the groups working at the Presbyterian Church of the Covenant in Boston and the Summerfield United Methodist Church in New Haven, Connecticut. It is an option in some denominations where entire congregations are commissioned for their special ministries once a year, and in places where there is a clergy shortage.[22]

This possibility of variety and of corporate pastorates is going to become ever more important because of the number of women entering the seminaries. The Association of Theological Schools reports that from 1972 to 1977 the enrollment of women increased 118.9 percent and of men only 20.2 percent.[23] The entrance of large numbers of women into ordained ministry may cause it to become *a female profession* like nursing or primary school teaching. Sexism causes work done by women to be devalued in society, and when large numbers of them enter a field the men tend to leave and the prestige and salaries drop. If this prejudice continues, it may cause ordained ministry, which is already associated with the private sphere and with feminine cultural characteristics of being loving and kind, to become not only "feminized" but also "female." This might have a side benefit in causing the erosion of the last status associated with being clergy so that the line between clergy and laity would disappear. Yet this would not be a change leading to new forms of partnership in the congregation if the congregation is simply abandoned to the care of only one half of the human family, as seems to have happened in the case of the nuclear family.

These are not the only possible changing roles in ministry. However, they point us toward some of the problems and possibilities that we might experience as we seek to move beyond the clergy and laity split among the people of God in order to set both groups free to use their talents in the service of God and humanity.

MINISTRY AND PARTNERSHIP

The church today needs new life-styles in ministry. We must go back to hearing anew what the Bible says to us about our calling to service. But we must also go forward with experimental life-styles that seek to overcome old dichotomies that we have inherited: clergy/laity, male/female, rich/poor, black/white, gay/straight, if we are to discover again the *One Calling* of God as partners with Jesus Christ.

Vocation is God's address to each of us, something we all share, regardless of our walk of life. As we search for ways to respond to God's call, each of us will find different responses and different contexts, but the same vocation to journey toward freedom and wholeness in Jesus Christ. The ministry is part of that one call as each and every Christian is set free for others, set free to serve *now* in and through many communities and situations. Only as we see clearly that vocation and ministry are *not* options for *some* Christians, but are basic to the existence of *all* Christians, can we begin to make choices that might open up future and hope for the many needs of God's groaning and longing world.

There is general theological agreement that Biblical witness to vocation and ministry indicates one calling to service for all Christians and that the *laos* (whole people of God) were indistinguishable from the *klēros* (those who will inherit). This agreement also extends to the consensus that the ministry of Christ as Prophet, Priest, and King is carried out by the whole people of God. Within this general calling the New Testament reflects a varied pattern of ministry, including that of president and deacon in Pauline churches and presbyters in the Palestinian churches.[24]

This variety of patterns of ministry continues in the history of the church with bishop, priest, monk, nun, theologian, pastor, preacher, and evangelist all still recognized as special ministries of those who have received gifts of the Spirit for the work of the church (I Cor. 12:27–31; Eph. 4:11–12).[25] In spite of the fact that the divisions between laity and clergy did not exist in the same way in the early church when organization was more fluid, and in spite of the fact that there has always been a variety of models for ministry, there is still a general acceptance of the idea of "special ministry" in whatever form this might take for a particular confession. In the words of the World Council of Churches' report on *One Baptism, One Eucharist and a Mutually Recognized Ministry:*

> The essential and specific function of the special ministry is: to assemble and build up the Christian community, by proclaiming and teaching the Word of God, and presiding over the liturgical and sacramental life of the eucharistic community.[26]

The implication of this is that provision for the proclamation and teaching of the Word and for the sacramental life of Christian communities is a vital part of church life. Any provisions for changes in clerical function would have to take account of this need, along with others that emerge as Christian communities seek to be faithful to their calling to participate in God's Mission and service in the world. But provisions for sharing of the Word and Sacraments, as well as for administration, can be made in different ways, for instance, as they have been in the Society of Friends and the Salvation Army. Changes are likely to come very slowly, not only because religious institutions change slowly but also because those who are in power in most church bodies are largely those clergy who presently hold the status and/or power that would have to be relinquished.

Suggestions for developing more equal partnerships in ministry must be made with the recognition that changes are difficult and risky for both the clergy and the churches. But changes are needed if we are to respond to the new challenges of the world today and to God's call to service in a New Age.

Eschatological Perspectives

When we look at ministry in the light of God's promised future, we can be confident that there *are* many ways to carry out the "impossible possibility" of service. Such service has never been easy and has always included the perspective of cross and suffering for those who share in serving with the outcasts and futureless people of society. Yet God's power to act on behalf of new human creation through our feeble efforts makes it possible for us to risk either acceptance of clerical ordination or refusal of it, as our "acceptable service" before God (II Cor. 8:12).

Whether or not we seek clerical ordination or are already ordained, in my opinion ordination should be for the purpose of subverting the "clergy line" and changing the structures of the church so that the whole people of God might once again find ways to exercise their spiritual gifts of service as those who anticipate the full partnership of the New Age. We can choose and have chosen various strategies and we can change our ways of working at different points in our lives. All of us can contribute to the same purpose if we remember that life is for service and not for earning power in various church systems.

We can accept clerical ordination because we need it to exercise our gifts in the place we are called to serve. Given the present structures of the church, there are some points at which new forms of partnership are possible only for those who are willing to accept certification as professional Christians. Some of us have completed or will complete our certification process and delay ordination because, at the moment, there is not clear necessity for it in the service we wish to perform, or because we are barred from ordination because of gender or sexual orientation. Many of us will choose or have chosen to express our calling and ministry, confirmed in Baptism, as so-called "laity." Here we can combine our spiritual gifts with other occupations that free us to serve the church and world in a variety of partnerships, not necessarily dependent on church institutions.

Whatever we choose or have chosen, the resulting functions and/or status in clerical or nonclerical ministry should be considered *hōs mē* (I Cor. 7). Our individual roles and relationships in the beginning of the New Creation are of penultimate importance. What is of ultimate importance is our calling to service in the name of Jesus Christ and the partnership that creates among us, as a new focus of relationship in sharing a common history in Jesus Christ that sets us free from ourselves and for others. The forms and roles of that relationship are *hōs mē* in a New Age with new signs of life-style. How one works out one's calling has always been situation-variable. For instance, even such an important person as John Calvin did not find it necessary ever to be ordained. And, of course, women in every age have found it possible to discover ways of service in the church though many of their gifts were ignored because they could not be ordained.

Perhaps at the present time an important eschatological sign of the New Age would be to create small Christian communities of service where the partnership clearly transcends the question of clergy-laity barriers. One such group of women and men living in community might be Sojourners in Washington, D.C. Another sort might be Roman Catholic women's orders and other women's groupings where there is deliberate sharing of gifts and avoidance of rigid hierarchy. Still another would be groups organized around social needs, such as health services, legal services, housing, and political advocacy who recognize and find ways to support and empower persons for the common task.[27]

One way to begin now to live out God's intended partnerships is to refuse to accept the divisions between laity and clergy. One group has done this by changing the language and speaking only of *laergy,* a combination of the words "laity" and "clergy." Writing on "Laergy: The Partnership Between Laity and Clergy at the Community of Hope Church in the Year 2000," a work group at Pacific School of Religion said of laergy:

> It indicates our belief that the church of the future must reflect the philosophical and theological realities of full partnership in Jesus Christ. For us, the word *laergy* (as in the case of synergy) denotes the combined energy of the lay-clergy relationship is greater than the sum of the energies of the individuals.[28]

The word "laergy" implies that the difference between laity and clergy can and will be eliminated and that each person must have the opportunity to contribute her or his gifts to the communal life we share in Christ. Changing language does not always change the reality but at least it reminds us of the reality of God's New Creation as we struggle to live out partnerships now as if they belonged to God's intended future.

God's Arithmetic

We saw in Chapter 1 that God's arithmetic in the New Age doesn't always add up in a quantitatively correct fashion. For instance, God seems frequently to work through "representative numbers." Not the many, and not those obviously suited by power and status to accomplish God's task, but the few, often those who are weak and of no account, become the instrument of God's mission. In the light of our analysis we could suspect that it is probably the "least" in the fellowship of believers who are most likely to become instruments of God's continuing redemptive action. It is not the clergy who are likely to be the representative numbers (contrary to much theology about "special ministry") in God's economy. It is the whole people in all their weaknesses that become, together, representatives of Christ's ministry.

This reversal of expectation is clear if we ask ourselves who is likely to be an instrument of liberation in any situation of oppression. It is the oppressed group which must respond to its call and identity and move to change the situation of oppression. It is they who must claim their own freedom, for when it is given by the oppressors it can also be taken back. Oppressor groups seldom go against their own self-interest and, therefore, it is only as the situation changes from below that they can be forced as a group to change the system that oppresses. This applies to the relationship of laity and clergy insofar as the laity are oppressed. They must move to see themselves as called to be God's representative number, and to share in a partnership of ministry. As they grow in the use of their gifts, perhaps God will use them as instruments to overcome the divisions between themselves and the church clergy.

If, in spite of fleeing from ministry, we find that it is important to seek clerical ordination in order to serve in a certain way, we need to remember that clergy are not the only representatives of God, nor are they able by virtue of their own position to be liberators of the laity. In my own experience, I worked to achieve a partnership in ministry with the staff and volunteer team ministry in the East Harlem Protestant Parish in New York City. This worked well and encouraged a sharing of gifts in the whole congregation as long as I as a clergyperson wanted us all to be partners. Yet the denominational structures had not changed and the laity were not sufficiently sure of their own independence. When I, the member of the oppressor group that had tried to "free the oppressed," was replaced by another clergyperson it was perfectly simple to return to the old divisions between first-class and second-class citizens in the church.

This particular situation illustrates some of the factors that need to be present in developing a partnership among individuals of differing education, skills, and social and ecclesiastical recognition. The persons find their focus of relationship in Jesus Christ, and their commitment to Christ and to the task of service at hand makes them equal members of the partnership. This equality and mutuality of support must be recognized by all the partners so that those who have less "status" can claim for themselves their own self-identity and worth.

The skills recognized and developed by the community depend on the needs of the ministry it sets out to accomplish. Depending on the particular needs of the situation, various persons would be called to develop certain of their spiritual gifts, even when this requires additional training for those with less formal, professional education.

The various spiritual gifts in a partnership are not equal, for the Spirit acts in many ways, but a community of support can emerge and grow as one plus one becomes three or more. In this way an ever-wider group begins to share in the partnership and the persons who are not recognized by ecclesiastical structures or social structures will continue to receive support from one another. This would be essential if a particular clergyperson leaves the partnership and others are not sure they can continue the ministry.[29] Members of oppressed groups, no matter where they seek to serve, continue to need a strong support network for their work in order to affirm their particular gifts.

There are ways to avoid the temptations of clerical ordination. One of them is to seek positions in the life of the church that keep one sufficiently *marginal* to retain a critical perspective of what is happening and not simply to give in to human arithmetic. This might be the case if one worked in a cultural setting where one did not fit so that it was necessary always to learn from others; or if one continued to be involved in some area outside the church that questioned the faith stance of the church; or if one was in some position in a congregation that had low status and little power such as that of Christian education minister. In these cases it would be easier to remember that one of the primary roles of any clergyperson today is that of nurture and enabling so that the ministry of God's representatives might multiply.

Other functions that clergy might serve in order to become advocates of laergy might be that of "holding up the system" so that those whose talents are smothered and oppressed by it can find "room to breathe" and to use those gifts. Or that of sharing the resources of the tradition so that all of the people can learn to "do theologically" whatever they do. In this, as in any ministry, it is of course essential that one have the strength to be oneself rather than play roles that defeat the authentic service of a woman or man seeking to share with others as representatives of God's care.

In this day and age any form of ordination beyond baptism is an *extraordinary* call, one that we should accept only because we can imagine no other alternative. Like marriage, ordination is something you do only because you cannot imagine your life apart from that relationship with all its impossible possibilities. In the light of this chapter it certainly must be asked, *Why be ordained?* Such a question must be answered by each of us as we flee from ministry, and yet ultimately, perhaps, find ourselves saying, "I have to!" and find others saying, "Yes, we need you in this form of ministry!"

Flight from ministry has been around for a long time. The prophets were reluctant to respond to God's call. The disciples fled from the arrest and the cross. Fourth-century ministers knew it was an impossible job, one that they could do only because the One Minister, Jesus Christ, had already done it. For instance, Ambrose, a civil servant in Rome turned monk, actually hid from the church that elected him bishop. They had to capture him, ordain him, and make him bishop, for he was sure he could not do it!

The flight goes on and so does the question: Not, Why should women or gays or handicapped be ordained? but, Why should *anyone* try this impossibly possible form of service? Those who do choose to be ordained still have a long road ahead, for all of us keep hearing God's call and having to choose over and over how we will live out that call to freedom and service in the New Age.

7

LOVING THE QUESTIONS

In our search for alternative patterns of partnership we have seen that a key ingredient of human partnerships is that they are living, growing, and changing. A partnership is a new focus of relationship in which there is continuing commitment and common struggle in interaction with a wider community context. Even this very general working description which we have been using for our reflections forces us to consider how human beings learn to build partnerships that have ability to change and mature, and to change and end where necessary. Psychologists and social scientists of all kinds are constantly trying to find this out as they analyze changing patterns of relationships in our changing societies. Even churches have begun to recognize that partnerships of various kinds are not always for life, and liturgies of parting as well as coming together are needed.[1]

One important factor that contributes to committed and open partnerships is a real *love for questions.* Many of us fear questions. We are afraid that they will expose our ignorance or our guilt at the facade of our own shaky human relationships. Yet it is the willingness to admit ignorance and failure that makes it possible to go on learning and discovering new things. The excitement of discovering truth that is new to us in any sector of our lives can be a way of keeping ourselves and our partnerships growing. Large business partnerships employ people just to ask questions, and pay people to do all manner of change-related research. But even among a small group the same insight applies. Growth comes through loving the questions and learning from them. As Rainer Maria Rilke says in his *Letters to a Young Poet:*

I want to beg you, as much as I can, to be patient toward all that is unsolved in your heart and try to love the questions themselves like locked rooms and like books that are written in a very foreign tongue.[2]

Like children, adults continue to grow and change. Like children, they need to ask their way, to inquire and investigate. When a child does not grow this way we call it arrested development. When an adult stops growing and questioning we call it maturity![3] Certainly there is a problem here, a problem of arrested development in adults that can end partnerships by freezing them into one mold.

Some people may respond that talking about questions, alternatives, open future, and the like is a dangerous thing to do. It can lead into false paths, if the questions are wrong. It can lead to irresponsible answers based on selfish subjectivity. It can lead to paralysis of action and a long line of unanswered questions. Certainly any attempts to build new models of human relationships are risky and these and many other dangers are present. Those who experiment often get hurt and hurt others. But in a world in which we do not have answers and blueprints, loving the questions may at least provide a means of sharing in a partnership of learning how to journey together toward God's future. In any case those who choose to live as Christians have no choice about the journey without maps. For they, like Sarah and Abraham, have only the promises of God and not the answers.

As we search out additional ways we might grow as partners with God and one another, let us focus on the art of questioning, seen as partnership in a learning process in which we try to live the questions and thus to learn our way into the future.

PARTNERSHIP IN LEARNING

The basic reason one can love questions is not that questions themselves are so attractive. It is because of the *persons who ask questions* and think about them, persons given us by God in many places and situations as partners in learning. Not only do we constantly discover questions in our own lives as persons addressed by God to become what God intends, but also we discover the most interesting life situations in which persons and their actions raise questions.

Christian theology itself is a way of questioning God and being questioned. We use our mind *(logos)* to understand how God *(theos)* is known to us through the Word in the world. This is done in partnership with others of all ages and places in the unfinished task of understanding the question of the Gerasene demoniac in Mark 5:7, "What have you to do with me, Jesus, Son of the Most High God?" Theology is thus a partnership in learning; learning who we are as addressed by God, and by others.

In the same way education, whether it takes place as a form of personal or social growth, happens as *partnership in learning.* The process of education is one of actualizing and modifying the development of the total person in and through dialogical relationships.[4] What has happened to many of us is that the focus of our education has been in school systems that have taught us to be *not partners but competitors,* not questioners of the *status quo* but conformists to our class, sex, race, and assigned socioeconomic destiny. This inheritance has long since been exposed as *miseducation,* but it is still the dominant mode of school systems around the world, including those concerned with professional theological education.[5]

In order to become partners with one another in life, we need remedial education that will help us form the sort of open and caring attitudes that help partnerships to flourish. In his book *Creative Ministry,* Henri Nouwen has called the two styles of education "teaching as a violent process" and "teaching as a redemptive process."[6] The contrast has been described by many educational reformers as moving from teaching as imparting subject matter to others toward learning as a self-actualizing experience of growth. For instance, Ivan Illich, in *Deschooling Society,* discusses an open-ended exploration best nurtured through matching partners who share a common agenda and puzzlement together and begin to explore.[7] Paulo Freire contrasts "deposit making" and "problem posing education" in *Pedagogy of the Oppressed.*[8]

Using Nouwen's concept of violent versus redemptive teaching, we can see that violent teaching fails to model and to facilitate the art of partnership. It is *competitive* in fostering fear among students and between students and teacher, *unilateral* in its information flow, and *alienating* in separating students from the real world for which they are supposed to be preparing.[9] Teaching as a redemptive process provides the possibility of learning the art of partnership by allowing people to be partners in learning. It assists the process by being *evocative* in encouraging the sharing of life experiences, *bilateral* with joint learning of teacher and students, and *actualizing* in modeling present behavior that relates to the wider community.[10] As Nouwen says:

> In this case schools are not training camps to prepare people to enter into violent society but places where redemptive forms of society can be experimented with and offered to the modern world as alternative styles of life.[11]

Such a style has been used in seminaries where an effort is made to model teamwork and shared learning by involving students together with faculty and field resource persons in joint efforts of action-reflection. One such program in which I participated was made up of small groups, each with two resource persons: a faculty member and a local pastor, social worker, pastoral counselor. The teams of two worked with student groups on both theological content and experiential sharing from personal and field placement questions and insights. Four of those small groups met simultaneously so that the eight resource persons could plan jointly for common meetings of the larger group that would include give-and-take among resource people as well as students. Such an attempt to break the "academic/practical" separation and to model inclusive teamwork among people of various sexes, races, and backgrounds is especially important for pastoral education. Many students will need to learn to minister *with* others and not just *to* or *at* them. One of the most powerful learning tools is the teaching model presented, which is later used "violently" or "redemptively" by those who have shared in such an experience.[12]

Participation in God's Actions

Education as a growth process is always participatory. Those who seek to be involved in learning the meaning of their Christian faith find themselves drawn into what is called Christian or theological education. Here persons find themselves as partners in learning through participation in God's actions. Over the years I have reflected in different contexts and situations on the meaning of education as part of the intentional process of learning about God as God is known in the world. As I look back I notice that the context changes the wording, yet, in every case, there is an affirmation of my faith and my life experience that Christian education or nurture has to do with God's initiative, and our partnership or participation, together with others, in an ongoing process.

In the early 1960's, as a pastor in East Harlem I described Christian education as "participation in Christ's invitation to join in God's Mission of restoring us to true humanity."[13] In the late 1960's in writing on the meaning of "Tradition as Mission," I came to talk of it as joining God's traditioning action as God hands over Jesus Christ into the hands of coming generations and nations.[14] In the early 1970's I was teaching Christian education and doing ecumenical work with the YWCA. I described education as: participating in God's stewardship (*oikonomia*, I Cor. 9:17), in building up (*oikodomē*, Eph. 4:11–16; I Cor. 3:10–11) the household (*oikos*, Gal. 3:27–28) of God for the whole inhabited world (*oikoumenē*, Phil. 1:27).[15] In the mid-1970's I was to describe liberation education as action-reflection on "the meaning of oppression in the light of our participation in God's creation of a fully human society."[16]

In this context of struggling to see how Christian education relates to our partnership together in God's action, it would seem that it is consistent with the other descriptions to speak of education as *partnership in learning.* Because God has chosen to be partners with us, we can learn the meaning of God's love and service in our lives. Because we find communities of believers, both past and present, who have been partners in learning to share God's love, we can ourselves grow and be nurtured. Because there are persons willing to risk opening their lives to us and with us, we can risk asking questions about who we are and what God intends us to become. Therefore, participation in God's action clearly leads us to a partnership in learning that includes all the many ways we might want to describe this.

A key question that arises from this description is how Christian communities can become themselves authentic partnerships of learning and serving in order for learning to be "redemptive" and not "violent." Like educational institutions, churches have structures of organization and life-styles that often work against the understanding of redemptive learning. Only as we seek to provide authentic communities where faith is shaping life will we be able to help others discover the possibility of a partnership of learning.[17] Any process of education will be only as strong as the teaching and learning partnerships that provide the context for young and old to continue exploring their questions.

An example of the trend to provide resources for churches in expanding the areas and ways of nurture can be seen in the project of The Christian Church of Northern California–Nevada that provides a *Leadership Resource Directory.* This directory lists the names of resource persons in the entire area with their background and the type of skill they would bring and provides a way of matching partners for workshops and educational events of all kinds related to: Congregational Group Activities; Personal Life; Arts; Religion; Outreach and Social Concerns; Community Involvement; and Church Administration.[18] The entire network, which could easily be organized ecumenically, includes people of all walks of life and provides means of partnership and learning in many fields.

Liberation in Community

Education as a partnership in learning is a process of self-liberation in community with others. As the Final Assembly of the World Council of Christian Education in Lima, 1971, said:

> To educate is not so much to teach as it is to become committed to a reality in and with people, it is to learn to live, to encourage creativity in ourselves and others; and under God and [God's] power, to liberate [humanity] from the binds that pervert the development of God's image.[19]

This understanding has been elaborated by Paulo Freire in his writings and work in Geneva with the World Council of Churches. Certainly his pedagogy is one of emphasizing the process of learning to question one's world and to take action to change and humanize it. Education is seen as a process of liberation in community that includes "conscientization" as "learning to perceive the social, economic, political contradictions and to take action against the oppressive elements of reality."[20] He describes liberation itself as "a praxis of action/reflection of people on their world in order to transform it."[21]

The Fifth Assembly of the World Council of Churches entitled the Section on education, "Education for Liberation and Community." In the materials for the Section there was an effort to underline the fact that education in the church should be a sign of coming liberation in community by the way its members are educated to participate in God's actions in the world through the total context of its life.[22] More often than not, the community itself fails to manifest a partnership in mission that can be the liberating context for learning.

Nevertheless, in all parts of the world people are finding partners in and outside of the church in their struggle for human dignity. In affirming the possibility of a world of justice, equality, and freedom from want, they become partners working for an open future, negating the negative of present reality and refusing to settle for the *status quo* in their lives or in the lives of others. As they struggle together they become partners who share together in the journey of freedom because they seek to participate in some small way in shaping their future. They become self-actualizing human beings as they question their former roles as objects and as perpetuators of systemic violence, oppression, and manipulation.

Liberation in community helps us to remember that the separation of Christian education from other forms of education is a false dichotomy. Not only is education a total process of learning from the whole of life and, therefore, not just what happens in school or church school; education that leads toward Christ is a total process of learning that happens as the witnessing community shares as partners of all ages in reflection and study, and in action in the world. It is only as we join together to carry out the story of God's love for the world by our actions that education begins to be a partnership in learning between one another and God that sets us free to change ourselves and our world. The center of liberation in community for a Christian is Christ the Liberator, but the thrust of that liberation in community is on behalf of others as we follow the life-style of Jesus Christ.

LIVING THE QUESTIONS

In loving questions we look to persons who present them in actions and words as those who share with us in the experiment of life itself. For loving questions involves us in living them as well. They have no answers unless they are tried out and experimented with in thought, shared experience, and action. For instance, a woman may find herself confronted with the question, Who am I, what can I do? as her children begin to grow up and to leave home. She can try to escape the question in frantic activity, or she can learn from the writings and experience of others around her as well as from artistic expressions such as Doris Lessing's *The Summer Before the Dark*. But in order to find out what the answer to that question is, she must risk many more questions by trying out the alternatives she finds for living out her questions. In such a situation she may very well be so flooded with questions that she experiences "Question Shock." However the questions may arise, if they are important life questions, they will have to be *lived out*, and not just *figured out*.

Prefigurative Partnership

In her chapter from *Culture and Commitment*, entitled "The Future: Prefigurative Cultures and Unknown Children," Margaret Mead points us toward some important ways of keeping ourselves open to the future by living out our questions.[23] In summary, Mead is arguing

> that we have shifted from a culture that is "postfigurative" (one in which the young learn from the old) to one that is "cofigurative" (one in which both children and adults learn chiefly from their peers). She appeals for a "prefigurative" culture in which, as the future explodes into the present, the old learn from the young.[24]

According to Mead, the dimensions of change in our present world are unique and have produced new conditions around the globe. Everyone who was born and bred before the Second World War is an immigrant in time, unfamiliar with conditions of life in a new era and unable to communicate with the younger generation born into this new world.[25] The younger generation has turned to its peers for learning, but this has left culture in the hands of the still powerful elders, who in turn are threatened by rebellious youth. She suggests that we can learn and store knowledge in a new way if we develop prefigurative models in which adults teach their children "not what to learn, but how to learn and not what they should be committed to, but the value of commitment."[26] The young must ask the questions because they are the ones who understand the future which is already upon us. But enough trust must be reestablished so that the elders will be permitted to work with them on the answers.

Certainly Mead's suggestion for intergenerational partnership is a very important one that points the way beyond the old style of "top-down" learning and working toward a mutual sharing of gifts. This can happen only if those in authority are willing to show their weakness and to admit their need of sharing with the young, with teaching and learning going in both directions. One place to begin such a model is in the family, where it is possible, by recognizing that parents and children learn from each other, to work together at sharing of gifts and responsibilities so that eventually parents and children become partners in their explorations and life. Such partnerships that look expectantly for the right questions that can be lived out are crucial in a changing world, for, as Mead points out by quoting from *The Hamlet of A. MacLeish:* "We have learned the answers, all the answers: It is the question that we do not know."[27]

In a world of future shock the answers of our past alone do not suffice. We must also have the questions of our future that is even now breaking into our lives. These questions do not come only from young to old, or student to teacher. They come from every marginalized person and group which contradicts the assumed future by pointing to the oppressive realities of our world. These questions from those seeking a future to hope in are a key aspect of prefigurative learning if it is to assist us in building an open future for all.

One of the difficulties in building new processes of dialogue and communication is that the voiceless must themselves begin to name and change their world together with others. Too often the person in authority decides as teacher, pastor, official that everyone will participate in decision-making as a team. This in itself tries to establish partnership through authoritarian action. Those "made" partners have still to take their own power and to raise their own voices or there is partnership in name only.

There are many settings, however, in which one finds oneself in a position of *structural authority* simply by the role definition and power of the particular function. In such a setting a pastor, teacher, parent, or boss can try to resign the structural authority, but this does not necessarily help to create an alternative model for relationships. One way of altering the dynamic is by working toward a new position of shared *sapiential authority*.[28] People can be asked to turn to themselves and to one another for the particular wisdom that they can share, so that the one in charge is "in charge" only if he or she has the necessary sapiential authority or wisdom for the task at hand. This in turn may convince people that they can risk using their own life experiences, questions, and actions as the basis of interaction, because the focus is on wisdom contributed and not on the one "assigned" to be wise. Prefigurative partnerships are most certainly based on this form of sapiential authority and may assist us in thinking our way toward a future of new relationships.

Acting Our Way Into Thinking

Living the questions does not mean that there are no answers. It simply means that the clues and answers from the past have to be lived out critically in the present along with any clues we can gain from the future. As we seek to know the future through the new questions that constantly come to our lives, we discover that many of our old questions are answered or lead to a clarification of what the right questions might be. Often we are asking the wrong questions and therefore receive answers that do not lead us in the best direction, or that lead to a further, more basic question.

An example of this is one of the questions currently being asked about clerical ordination which were discussed in Chapter 6. Here we saw that a preoccupation with the question, Should women be ordained? concealed the more basic question about the nature of ordination itself, Why should anyone be ordained? The question of how to work out models for male and female clergy team ministry conceals a next question, which is how one moves from a clerical team to a team that includes the gifts of the whole people of God.

Often we have to live out the questions before we see that there are also other questions and other understandings of reality. Another way of describing this is to speak of *acting our way into thinking.* All of our thinking is colored by our life experience and that of those around us. Our theology, our educational theory, our values are expressed in certain ways because of clues we have gathered from the past. Henri Nouwen has underlined this by closing his reflections on *Creative Ministry* with a list of unanswered questions and observations made by people with different experiences. One way to change our thinking and questions is to seek out new experiences in which we come to act differently and to see reality in a different light. If we have a deep prejudice against blacks or women or gay persons, nothing short of actually sharing in new life experiences as equals with those persons or groups will cause us to question our assumptions. Even here we will resist this change by saying that the new experience is an exception unless others around us help raise our consciousness about what is happening.

An important means of "acting our way" is to be exposed to learning in a culture or subculture other than one's own. This is crucial if persons are to discover what it is to live with culture shock, to feel lost and marginal, and to be dependent on others who have far more sapiential authority in every way than they do in that setting of new language and new cultural signals. If it is not possible to go to another country, it is possible to live in a different subculture, economic bracket, or region in one's own country. This enables us to discover how conditioned we are by our own environment and become intentionally free from it in order to become partners with others from different backgrounds. In a summer school a student who spends most of his or her time on a small part in a play that is being put on in a black neighborhood will see everything else he or she is doing in a new light.[29] Students or family who spend one to three years working in a Third World country not only find out problems firsthand but find out a great deal more about themselves. Learning can be mutual for those who share cultures as a student, a Peace Corps or VISTA worker, a fraternal worker, or a volunteer.

Another aspect of partnership in learning is the importance of continuing education that emphasizes lifelong learning in which people share in deciding what they learn and engage in learning in relation to their own needs and those of their own community. Certainly any formal designs for learning would emphasize what Gregory Battenson has called *fourth level* learning.[30] The first two levels are learning facts and how to interrelate them. The *third level* is the most typical form of education in industrial society: learning to improve performance within existing systems of social understanding. In such a style the rewards are external and grades are used to prepare persons for external rewards of money later on. The fourth level includes all the others but goes farther by assisting persons to perceive the nature of present systems and to reexamine them with a view to discovering how a total system might be changed. This learning emphasizes subjective satisfaction. It comes close to the dimensions of liberating education and depends on the type of partnership in learning that Mead urges in her discussion of prefigurative culture.

We can be well informed without taking action. But taking action on any matter will provide the feedback likely to change the prior information and questions. Third level thinking fostered in educational styles often encourages a *false liberalism* in which people are taught to understand all sides of the matter. With this ability they remain neutral and do not risk taking action or making a stand on a personal or public issue. Information is gained with insight and understanding of human, political, and social problems, but the problems remain because of inactivity in the name of liberalism. Such inactivity is a vote for things to continue as they are. As Freire points out, it is mere *verbalism;* for thinking without action is verbalism, and action without thinking is activism.[31]

Fourth level thinking would be fostered in educational styles of action-reflection that assist persons to test out their insights and knowledge through action. A person able to do this, living with the questions and working toward humanizing changes, is in the process of *truly liberal* education or liberation to act and think in such a way as to contradict the dominating and destructive "reality" of our world.

LEARNING AND FUTURE

The future is a common theme in the partnerships of those who see that "life is for learning" in order to be self-actualized for others. Education as partnership in learning is the way in which we seek out models of open partnerships, for it is by experiencing such partnerships in family, school, church, and society that people catch sight of a future in which the hierarchical structures of domination and subjugation are overcome. In spite of many failures, it is still possible to struggle and risk together so that small signs of God's intended future of full partnership can be seen as an *impossible possibility* in the present. In the face of the social crises of our time we are called to relocate the future in the present by living out new prefigurative models of learning and building those into our social relationships now.

Eschatological Perspectives

"Facts are facts," many of us in this pragmatic, postmodern world are fond of saying. Yet we know that facts are often *not* facts. Reality is perceived differently by different people and the facts change. In interpersonal relationships this is painfully obvious when it comes to hearing the different descriptions of the same event that a particular man or woman might give.[32] Even so-called scientific facts are subject to the question asked and the interpretation given of the evidence. Otherwise we would not have moved, for instance, from Newton to Einstein in physics.

In the Biblical story this relativity of "facts" is very clear, for the facts do not have the last say. There is a reality of "feast" beyond the facts as we perceive them. For example, if we look at Isa. 25:6–9 we can see an example of the way feast is played off against fact, as well as fact against feast. For they come together in a new reality of God's feast of liberation for all nations.[33]

> On the Holy Mountain the Lord of all power will prepare a banquet for all peoples, a feast of superb wine, of delicious food. All the people could not see things as they really are; they had, as it were, a veil before their faces; these veils will be destroyed; their ideologies will be done away.

God will be victorious over death, forever! The Lord God will
wipe away tears from all eyes. God will make it come to pass that
even Israel will no longer be a scandal on the face of this earth.
And people will say; Look here, now, this is what we mean by
"God"! We have waited, hoping that God would liberate us: And
there God is, the Lord. We have waited for God. Now let us be
glad and celebrate our liberation! (Isa. 25:6–9)[34]

The Biblical message often plays off feast against fact. In verse
6 of Isaiah 25 we have a description of the banquet that God will
prepare for all nations, all the groupings of people in the world.
This is a feast of delicious food and superb wine, a feast of
abundance for all. The symbolism here is hard to miss. God's
creation is one that provides for all to share its bounty. This is
God's intended arithmetic and the way it is to become, exile and
starvation and all the rest notwithstanding.

The Hebrew people institutionalized this meaning of the future in a piece of what Hans Hoekendijk sometimes called
Zion's fiction. We see this Zion's fiction described in the institution of the Jubilee Celebration in Leviticus 25.[35] Here it is said
that every Fiftieth Year is a year of release. Everything that
belongs to God: people, property, land— *all* is returned to God
so it can be shared. Jubilee is a time to begin again and to share
the blessings as one people. It is possible that this image was in
the mind of Luke as he wrote Acts 2, the story of Pentecost, for
the gift of the Spirit was a signal that the New Age of unity and
restoration had come. As the story goes, there was such a star-
tling display of unity among the people that those in the so-
called "real world" could only think that the participants from
all the nations were drunk.

Such an experience of God's Jubilee comes to us when exodus
is spelled out again and again in terms of social and personal
salvation: of release from the facts of bondage through national
deliverance, achievements of equal rights and justice, or personal freedom from a dehumanizing situation. When we recall
such times in which shared hope and vision have become a
reality, we celebrate them as important clues of our longed-for
future. Such a moment of remembering that also points to the
future is the Lord's Supper, commemorating the life, death, and
resurrection of our Lord until he comes.

Yet if the Biblical message often plays off feast against fact, most of the messages of our world seem to go the other way. Fact is played off against feast. There is a recognition of this in verses 7 and 8 of Isaiah 25, which speak of veils and death as facts that will be overcome. People are unable to see things as they really are, for they see reality through the veils of custom, prejudice, ideology, so that they don't even know how to ask the questions that might lead to a future of wholeness and unity. The reality of God and of our neighbor is veiled in our own ideologies and fears. Partnership appears more as a hope than as a reality.

Death in many forms surrounds us and, until the facts of death, conflict, oppression, and disease are done away with, we still live in the Babel era and not that of Pentecost, the time of cross and not resurrection. No Jubilee appears over the horizon. Nations (even denominations) have a hard time speaking with one another, taking away all reproaches between them. Women and men still have not been able to listen deeply enough to one another so that they can share one new reality that overcomes structures of domination.

The facts are facts and are present as we prepare the table in the presence of all sorts of enemies: incredible affluence built on the exploitation of others; unbelievable suffering wrought by racism; fear, alienation, and domination built into our closest daily relationships in family, work, church, and government. Against these facts the feast of the Holy Mountain and all our talk of partnership as a *new* focus of relationship looks more like a mirage than a substantive banquet. God's liberation looks like a utopian dream.

Yet the Biblical story talks about "opening the eyes of the blind" (Luke 4:18). It invites us to a feast of liberation that is not just a dream. It is an anticipation of a new reality breaking in as we, like Israel, hope against hope. We hope in God because God hopes in us and we can celebrate God's hope as we respond to the call to live out the promise in our lives. We are already on our way as we break bread and pour the wine in the New Age. In playing off the feast of liberation against the facts of bondage, we are joining God's protest movement by sharing in a foretaste of the feast and living out that vision of partnership *(koinōnia)* in our lives. "We have waited for God. Now let us be glad and celebrate our liberation" (Isa. 25:9).

God's Partnership

God's partnership with us frees us to ask questions and to hope expectantly in the new possibilities of our lives. Living according to a different arithmetic, in new relationships of service for others, often makes us misfits in the world of fact, but this is what our partnership is about. We belong to God and not just to the reality described by others around us, and because of this we respond to the questioning of God about how we are living out the story of Jesus of Nazareth in our partnerships. In turn, we question not only ourselves but also the way things are in the light of what God intends them to become (Luke 4:18–19; Rom. 8:18–27; Isa. 25:6–9; 43:18–21).

Jesus saw that his disciples had forgotten his teaching and example of service and had begun to ask the wrong questions when they came to him and said, "Who is the greatest in the kingdom of heaven?" (Matt. 18:1). His answer was to place a child in their midst and say, "Whoever receives one such child in my name receives me" (v. 5). Here and in the accounts of Luke 9:46–48 and Mark 9:33–37 the implication is that all outcasts and misfits, including children, women, handicapped, old, and poor, are welcome in God's New Age. It is in solidarity with all humanity that we include the outsiders in the story of God's love and thus invite them into a partnership of learning and living. Such learning between children and adults, women and men, rich and poor, sick and healthy, black and white is not only prefigurative, it is also eschatological. It prefigures the end toward which we hope, where all can share their gifts.

This end may seem far away, because, like the disciples, we often go astray and begin to ask the wrong questions. But in spite of our own weakness and failures God is a hopeless optimist about us, calling us over and over again to righteousness and faithfulness. It is this *incurable optimism of God* that gives us *a future to hope in* as we become partners in learning, loving the questions and living them out in our shared communities of action and reflection. As we wait actively with patience (Rom. 8:25) we may be helped in our journey to remember the words of Rilke:

Do not now seek the answers which cannot be given you because you would not be able to live them. And the point is, to live everything. Live in the questions now. Perhaps you will gradually, without noticing it, live along some distant day into the answer.[36]

PART III

BEGINNING FROM THE OTHER END

Some books begin with the theological rationale and methodology that underlies the research of the author. Here, however, the *beginning is at the other end.* There is no one "right place" for such a chapter when we view theology as a continuing process of action-reflection. Placing it at the end may assist in reflecting on the meaning of the previous discussion on partnership. At the same time the chapter points ahead to other possible uses of an eschatological perspective.

In Jesus Christ, God has chosen to be partner with us in our world and lives. That choice is known to us in a "memory of the future." We remember the story of God's love and live out that story, moving with hope in the promised future of New Creation. The other end of the story draws us into God's future and illuminates our present journey.

8

PARTNERSHIP AND THE FUTURE

One of the most pressing questions of our time is whether partnership has a future at all. In a world changing so fast, people, marriages, churches, nations, and economies are in danger of flying apart. It was such a context as this which led those who attended the Fifth Assembly of the World Council of Churches in Nairobi, 1975, to consider it an achievement to have acted out the theme, "Jesus Christ Frees and Unites," at least to the extent of *staying together* as a Council of Churches.[1] They looked at all the centrifugal forces tearing themselves and the world apart and were able to affirm that in the midst of destruction there is still hope for God's liberating action; and, in the midst of division, there is hope for communion, for partnership in Jesus Christ.

It is the affirmation of this book that partnership does have a future, just as it has a present and a past. It has a future because God has chosen to be partners with us, chosen to be present in our lives through Jesus Christ as a happening of cohumanity. Furthermore, it is God's intended future of new creation in community that gives us clues to what partnership means.

The question of partnership presents itself to us for serious action and reflection not only because of what seem to be ever-increasing possibilities of "falling apart," but also because we are confronted on every side by the question: "After equality, what?"[2] After we struggle toward freedom and equality of race, sex, and class, how do we live out that equality? What does equal partnership look like? In pursuing such an investigation we must look more closely at a new revolution of consciousness in which it may be possible that everyone can win. And then, in the light of this we can search for some provisional descriptions of future and partnership as a context for our theological reflection.

A REVOLUTION IN WHICH EVERYONE WINS

In his book *The Feminine Factor*, Eric Mount suggests that the women's liberation movement may lead to the liberation of men as well. Paraphrasing the peace slogan, "What if they gave a war and nobody came?" he asks, "What if they gave a revolution and everybody won?"[3] There is such a possibility present in the changing consciousness of women and men about their life-styles and roles in society. And if it happened that people learned to live more humanly and cooperatively, surely that would be a "revolution of freedom" in which people could dwell together in a new house of freedom. This would constitute a further stage in the list of freedom movements described by Jürgen Moltmann in *Religion, Revolution, and the Future:*

> The freedom movements based on Christian faith, on the church, on the conscience, on the citizen and Socialism have succeeded one another in such a way that the one caught fire in the disappointing consequences of the preceding one as each strove for greater freedom. So far, no one of them has brought about the "realm of freedom" itself, but each one has opened a new front in the struggle for freedom.[4]

Changing Social Structures

In an interdependent world of six continents we find ourselves located in many cultures and social configurations. All of these contexts are important settings for the development of our understanding of partnership, but for the purposes of this particular study I underline the continuing and dynamic process of changing human consciousness by looking at this development in Western societies.[5]

Western culture is rooted in a fusion of Jewish and Hellenistic culture expressed in the so-called synthesis of *medieval* society. In this society the world was viewed as anchored in a unified religious tradition. Ideas were expressed through past-oriented myths, and technology was preindustrial. In the *modern*, or industrial, society there developed a variety of world views, emerging from the different economic units formed to serve industrial specialization. Ideas were often expressed through future-oriented ideologies.

In a *postmodern* or postindustrial society, Western culture and other cultures influenced by Western technology have become ever more pluralistic and yet more homogenized and unified through communications networks and multinational trade networks. Society functions, not through established orders of creation or even through separate human institutions, but through interlocking systems of institutions. Widespread searching for meaning in a rapidly changing world leads to nihilism and hedonism, as well as to a return to ideologies and religions. Yujiro Hayashi, a Japanese futurologist, describes this radical shift:

> As the Industrial Revolution signaled a transformation of preindustrial society into industrial society, we are now on the verge of accomplishing a new transformation of great historical significance: the transformation of industrial into postindustrial society. The social changes produced by this transformation will far exceed in magnitude changes experienced at the time of the Industrial Revolution, for what is implied is a complete overhaul of society's basic values.[6]

There is no way of knowing in what direction social structures will evolve, for history always has surprises in store for us. Nor do people or groups find themselves only in one type of world view or culture. We often commute from postmodern to medieval attitudes or values in the space of a few hours, and people can be found living in various places in ways that are more characteristic of an earlier period. Yet it is clear that history in general has been shaped by these cultural trends.

As we look back, it is possible to discern the end of the medieval system in the French Revolution and the Industrial Revolution and responses to these events such as the Communist Manifesto of 1848. We can also see that the end of the industrial era came shortly after the Second World War around the 1950's and that there has been an accelerating pattern of change. Of course many events, large and small, have gone into the basic shifts, and any study of history can identify inventions, events, and persons who contributed to them. One such change important for the erosion of medieval society was the Reformation, in which the medieval synthesis of a unified church as provider of security in a unified society was challenged. A change that appears to be part of the development of post-industrial society is a new revolution of consciousness that may bring about a New Reformation in the church if not in all of society.

Revolution of Consciousness

The struggle of the women's liberation movement to overcome systemic oppression that makes one half of society inferior at birth is a struggle against dualism and alienation between and within persons and institutions. The struggle is basically for a *new human being:* one that is whole; that moves beyond social stereotypes of masculine and feminine, dominant and subordinate, to an understanding of human sexuality that recognizes the variety of sexual characteristics in each person.

Many people are pointing to this particular revolution of freedom as one that is important for all humanity. For instance, Janet Chafetz says that the future of the species depends on population control, preventing ecological deterioration, and avoiding war. To accomplish this, age-old notions of masculine and feminine must be fundamentally altered. Major social institutions reflect and support sex role stereotypes and profit from them:

> To the extent that such stereotypes significantly change, our institutions will be altered in profound ways. In short, such changes, if they occur, will constitute a veritable "revolution."[7]

Rosemary Ruether and Eugene Bianchi are pointing to the same thing in their book.[8] Ruether says that patriarchal culture is not a viable future for survival of humankind:

> This is a period when the women's movement, properly understood, encompasses all other liberation movements, [for all the ideologies of race, sex and class] . . . are the cultural superstructure for a system of male domination which is socioeconomic and systemic in character.[9]

Human beings are historical and changing. They become in many respects what they understand themselves to be. What we see among us is a new person, a new human being struggling to be born. This is causing a revolution, not only in our own homes, churches, or businesses, but also in the way human sciences are written and taught, the way the arts are pursued, and the way theology and ethics are developed.[10]

These dangerous generalizations about change are not simply "rhetoric." They represent the genuine aspirations, the "ferment of freedom," in the lives and hearts of large numbers of women and not a few men. The manifestations may be different in the West than in some other parts of the globe, but the growing awareness of false dualisms and destructive male myths of strength and dominance is apparent. In situations of political oppression, extreme racism, or poverty, women and men make survival their first agenda, but they look to a world where, in Dorothee Soelle's paraphrase of the Magnificat,

> the rule of males over females will come to an end
> objects will become subjects who
> win their own and better right.[11]

Whether this new wave of consciousness is strong enough to carry men and women to a new and deeper awareness of their relationship with themselves, one another, and the world remains to be seen. Women are still seeking out the meaning of their own self-identity as women, but many are aware that this must be accompanied with the risk of new mutuality with men if the process is to continue. There has emerged a new *paradigm of consciousness* which very slowly begins to work a revolution in the meaning of partnership in our society. This is underlined by Margaret Farley:

> In any case, for many persons profound conceptual and symbolic shifts have occurred in relation to gender differentiation and roles. Indeed, so profound are these changes and so far reaching their consequences that one is tempted to say that they are to the moral life of persons what the Copernican revolution was to science or what the shift to the subject was in philosophy.[12]

FUTURE AND PARTNERSHIP

In the face of a revolutionary change in consciousness and relationships, the question of how and in what context we can reflect theologically becomes very important to those of us whose life and faith are rooted in the love of Jesus Christ.[13] Certainly many of our clues will come from the past and present as we catch glimpses of what it might mean to be fully and newly human partners. At the same time, however, they must be guided by questions that are future-oriented in order to help our considerations be open to changing consciousness and perceptions.

Meaning of Partnership

We can speak of the future of partnership in at least three senses. First, there is future as the possibility of new life-styles and ways of being partners in marriage, friendships, business, church. Secondly, there is the future of society and the continued existence of humankind. In this sense we must learn to be newly and creatively human and to care for one another and the world, living together as copartners, or we will destroy ourselves and the world. Lastly, there is the future that is God's. This is the eschatological future: the goal or purpose of life that is prefigured in the coming of Christ and opened up by the promise and actions of God.

All of these futures are in a dynamic relation in any discussion of partnership for Christians, yet it is the third, the eschatological future, that provides a basic context for our theologizing. It is eschatology that provides, according to Moltmann, a "belief that takes the initiative toward transforming the world by means of the possibilities of the present."[14] This future perspective can help to overcome all forms of dualism by moving from future wholeness toward present human transformation.[15] It can also help us to focus on God's promised future of justice, freedom, and wholeness in order to catch the vision needed to understand new perspectives on the meaning of partnership with God. The *adventus,* God's future that comes toward us, breaking into our lives as the anticipations of God's intended creation, provides clues for partnership not just in Old Creation but in the New Creation begun in Christ.

As William McNamara has said, "Christ came not to start a new religion but a new world."[16] In Christ we have a change in the reality of our relationships, and it is the Christ event, past and present and future, that helps to shape our lives and partnerships as part of New Creation. The future as the context of our discussion of partnership is not utopian in the sense of no person's place *(outopia)*. It certainly is utopian in the sense of a good place for persons *(eutopia)*. What Moltmann calls the prolepsis or anticipation inherent in the Christ event makes present our future under conditions of alienation and oppression. As we are drawn toward God's intended future we can see "that God is not our utopia, but that we are God's 'utopia.' We are hoping for God, because [God] hopes for us."[17] Because of God's hope for us we search out the meaning of partnership, not as a new ideology, but rather out of trust in God's promised future, and we are willing to live with a poverty of knowledge about our future because of that trust.

Theology and Changing Consciousness

According to Max Warren, "Partnership is an idea whose time has not yet fully come, . . . but at least the birth-pains have begun."[18] There is a new recognition that survival of the world depends on pushing for new forms or fragmentary anticipations of shared community. As an important part of this trend, a new paradigm of consciousness about who we are as female and male in partnership is surely going to have an effect on theological reflection. Searching for ways in which society should be ordered to overcome previous patterns of dominance is going to raise questions about much of the patriarchal Biblical and church traditions on which Christian theology has been built. It will also raise questions about styles of theology that fail to include a wide variety of persons, both male and female, as partners in discussion. It will become less and less possible to continue exclusive practices in which dominant white, Western males set the "standards" for all other theologies.

Such a revolution of thinking is one in which those customarily on the receiving end (nonmale, nonwhite, nonstraight, non-Western) begin to make their own contributions out of their own contexts. This calls for nothing short of what Juan Luis Segundo describes as *The Liberation of Theology*. [19] The beginning of such a revolution is the awareness that God, salvation, judgment, sin, the powers of this world, are not perceived in the same way by those who have different experiences of that reality. Doctrinal answers handed down by one group are no longer normative descriptions of life and behavior for everyone. Rather, they represent accumulated wisdom out of *particular cultural contexts.* No one person writing theology out of a particular set of life experiences can interpret the meaning of the gospel for all others. Even our earliest accounts of the earthly Jesus come to us out of different faith communities in four different Gospels.

The gospel message itself is conveyed to us as stories of God's active love at work in Jesus Christ. This message is heard as good news by those who experience it in their own lives as deliverance. This hearing is situation-variable, for the liberating message is heard when it speaks to what particular groups of people seek to be free from and for. Jesus did not tell the blind they could walk, or the lame they could see, or the rich they could eat. He came to human beings where they were and sat where they sat, and out of that spoke to their inmost being. Through the power of the Spirit this is still possible in sharing the message today.

As we seek to speak and act God's Word we are each of us accountable not only to God and to the people of God in all centuries and in all places but also to those with whom we share a particular situation. With a shift in consciousness this is no longer simply the academic community or the parish church. Often it is a *community of struggle* out of which the action-reflection process of doing theologically whatever we do as Christians arises. The ecology of such theology is broadened to include the changing consciousness of a particular community of struggle that is seeking to find out what it would mean to live as partners in God's creation.

Not only does the liberation of theology involve understanding the contextual nature of all theology and rooting one's reflection in communities searching for new and liberating ways of partnership, it also calls for new models of *doing theology in partnership* so that the perspectives of one group help to challenge and raise questions for another as we seek to know the way God is at work in our lives. Questions raised by men and women growing up in a changed society can stand as critical corrections for those with more knowledge of the tradition, but little experience of the new consciousness. This can take place, however, only when each group or person is sufficiently sure of the respect and trust of the other that the dialogue goes on as a two-way process of mutuality.

Lastly, in the midst of changing consciousness and a rapidly changing world in which the future is now, the emphasis of such theology must be on the future of God that is breaking into our lives now. This *eschatological emphasis* would look to God's goal and purpose for life and creation as the basis for contradicting present reality when it is seen to be dehumanizing. In the name of the "new thing" God has been doing, is doing, and will do among women and men of all nations, a new partnership in theology may emerge in which a much more inclusive group of persons in many walks of life and culture share in telling their part in God's history of the future and hope. As Hans Hoekendijk has said,

> Christian hope . . . means that we move forward in a world with unlimited possibilities, a world in which we shall not be surprised when something unforeseen happens, but shall, rather, be really surprised at our little faith, which forbids us to expect the unprecedented.[20]

THEOLOGICAL PERSPECTIVES ON THE FUTURE

As women and men in a world of rapid and chaotic change we are called to focus our theological reflection not only on the past but also on the future. We have no choice but to take the future seriously, for the speed of change is such that both an unexamined past and an unexamined future operate as fate. As Christians we have another reason for looking to the future for our clues about present actions, and that is the Promise of God. In Jesus Christ the promise of New Creation has already broken into our lives and continues to lead us toward "a future and a hope" (Jer. 29:11).

It is crucial that we seek out the various alternative ways of reflecting on the meaning of the future in our investigation of partnership. The theological clues about new possibilities of partnership are to be found in the future perspectives of God's story with us. How we approach the future theologically will be an important factor in the questions we raise and the answers given.

The emphasis on eschatological themes is one of the shifts being brought about by the changing consciousness of the oppressed as they seek out the dimension of a new house of freedom. Although there is no one way to reflect eschatologically, it is helpful to know the various types of eschatology and to know why we might tend toward one particular approach in our interpretation of partnership.

In order to clarify ways of thinking about the future we will look more closely at some types of eschatology and then turn to a discussion of eschatological interpretation. Perhaps this will help us enter into the discussion of partnership with God and with others on a basis of mutual understanding.

Thinking About the Future

The future is an important theme in Biblical tradition and theology. Even before the events of the New Testament, the Hebrew people were thinking in a futuristic mode as they lived by faith in a God of promise whose redeeming action was known in the events of history. Christian theology and the future have always belonged together because the good news about Jesus of Nazareth is that God has decisively intervened in history and human life to establish the beginning of a New Age.

We can see the element of future in the New Testament writings which are apocalyptic in their view of the imminent end of the Age. In Mark 13 and parallels the material is called "The Little Apocalypse," for, like the book of Revelation, they use the thought patterns of their time to express the meaning of the coming of God's rule through tribulation and distress. The events of Jesus' own life and his teachings on the Kingdom of God reveal this same emphasis on the beginning of the New Age. Luke 4:19 speaks of Jesus' ministry as the proclamation of the "acceptable year of the Lord," a Year of Jubilee when the captives will be set free. The story of Pentecost is a reference to this same time of the outpouring of the Spirit when "your sons and your daughters shall prophesy, . . . and your old men shall dream dreams" (Acts 2:17; Joel 2:28–32). The Pauline epistles also reflect an urgency of the missionary task to tell the good news to all the nations at the close of the age (Rom. 8:18–22). The same motif appears in Matt. 24:14:

> And this gospel of the kingdom will be preached throughout the whole world, as a testimony to all nations; and then the end will come.

It can be said that apocalyptic is the mother of all theology because of the way it combines the question of God and the question of the future history.[21] But the styles of eschatology, or thinking *(logos)* about the end or goal *(eschaton),* have shifted over the centuries of Christian theology. In general we can identify four overlapping and not necessarily mutually exclusive approaches to eschatology: apocalyptic, teleological, axiological, adventological.

In the *apocalyptic* view the future is *imminent* because the end of the age and world is about to come to pass. As we have seen, this view of impending trials and tribulations in which the righteous will be vindicated by God is found in the New Testament as well as in Jewish writings of that period. Such an interpretation has continued to have strong emphasis in periods of history when there was a strong expectation of the immediate end of the world. Certain groups have stressed this view because of their emphasis on the work of the Holy Spirit, the urgency of missions, or strong millennial aspirations. However, during and after the New Testament period it tended to be modified to allow for the delay of the Parousia, or coming of Christ.

In its eventual preoccupation with establishing itself as a religion with creed, canon, and clergy the church tended to adjust its eschatology to this new situation by relegating it to the doctrine of last things, or teleology. The *teleological* view of the future as the *end* of life and the destiny of the soul was developed in theological writings and liturgies. Eschatology became the last chapter of systematic theology books which, in their composition, generally followed the order of topics in the creeds. Here the eternal destiny of the soul, death, and life after death were discussed. The focus on the future was the end of life and not just the end of the age.

The *axiological* view in which the future was depicted as

taking place *now* was developed at the end of the nineteenth century and the beginning of the twentieth century in response to modern Biblical criticism and historicism. Theologians such as the early Barth and Rudolf Bultmann shifted the emphasis away from teleology (things at the end, *eschata*) to axiology (emphasis on the center of personal history and the ultimate value or meaning of life in the present, *eschaton*). For Bultmann and others the eschatological views of the New Testament are closely allied with apocalyptic and, therefore, with mythological form. New Testament eschatology cannot be ignored and relegated to teleology because it is at the center of the gospel teachings of Jesus. For this reason the gospel must be interpreted so that it can be understood in the modern world through a program of demythologizing, realizing, and individualizing eschatology. For modern persons the value of life is here and now in the individual response of faith to the hearing of the Word of God. Such a view toward "realized" eschatology is not without precedent, for we can see the reinterpretation of the Parousia to refer to the faith of the believer already being developed in the Gospel of John, alongside the view that the New Age of the spirit is still to be completely fulfilled.

As variations of all three of these views continue to be held by Christians, the second half of the twentieth century has been a time of growing recognition of the socio-historical dimension of reality, and this has led theologians to take a new look at the future. This has led to the *adventological* view of eschatology in which the future is seen as the *new* that is coming into history. Such an emphasis was developed by such theologians as the later Barth, Moltmann, and Johannes Metz. In contrast to Bultmann, for instance, Moltmann was interested in remythologizing, futurizing, and socializing eschatology. That is, he was interested in the way that the apocalyptic myths could be spoken of in myths that opened up future and hope for the entire society and not just the individual. This view stresses, not the last things, or the ultimate meaning, but the Last One *(eschatos)*. Here eschatology becomes adventology because it is concerned with the One who comes to give meaning to history.

Along with all the other views, adventology contributes a different emphasis to the many and continuing theological discussions of the meaning of eschatology for the Christian faith.

These different emphases are presented as a typology in order to clarify ways of approach, not because any one way alone could do justice to the various dimensions of Biblical and Christian tradition. Nevertheless, it is the later view that informs the work of most of those doing political or liberation theologies. These theologies are concerned with understanding the liberating action of God in Christ in history as it is seen in the new possibilities of life, justice, and shalom. They look to the coming of Christ in and through the actions of Christians as they struggle to live out his suffering, solidarity, and resurrection through faithful actions in their lives.

Biblical Interpretation

The process of translation, explanation, or interpretation of the Bible is often called hermeneutics *(hermēneia)*. This word appears in the New Testament in Luke's story of how Christ began the process of interpreting the Old Testament in the light of the resurrection on the road to Emmaus (Luke 24:13–35).[22] It also appears in I Corinthians as Paul points out that the Spirit of Christ continues to grant gifts of interpretation in the church (I Cor. 12:10, 30; 14:5, 13, 27).

The use of hermeneutics in the Bible is frequently eschatological. The writers look at God's promised future in order to interpret and understand the past. They continue the process of tradition by interpreting the past in the light of the dimensions of the future that are opened up by events in history. Thus in Luke 24:13–35 Jesus points to the fulfillment of the promise in his own resurrection and interprets it anew so that the lives and actions of the disciples are changed.

An eschatological hermeneutic of the Bible in our own time would still have some of these elements found in Luke's resurrection narrative. The center of the interpretation process would be the self-revealing event in which Christ makes himself known among us in the breaking of bread and in the community that continues his Word and story through freely chosen life-styles of service. The interpretation would be a constant process of living out the story as a memory of the future and reflecting upon its meaning in relation to the Biblical account.

In seeking to develop a method of interpretation that can assist in formulating the eschatological message of the Bible under the conditions of the present situation of society, theologians have begun to focus on the relation of the understanding of faith to social practice.[23] In 1944, Dietrich Bonhoeffer wrote a baptismal message to his nephew, "For you thought and action will enter on a new relationship; your thinking will be confined to your responsibilities in action."[24] Today theologians such as Johannes Metz, Dorothee Soelle, José Miranda, Juan Luis Segundo, and José Miguez-Bonino are developing this insight.[25] They are seeking to work out a sociocritical hermeneutic that is critical not only of the historical situation of the Biblical texts but also of the present historical and theological realities. Thus Soelle says:

> The liberating significance of the historical critical method is lost whenever one disregards the hermeneutical circle and subjects past texts to historical-critical examination, but not one's own present and its problematic character as reflected historically in its origin and its dependence on social and psychosocial factors.[26]

The eschatological promises themselves of liberation, peace, justice, and reconciliation are promises of social well-being and not just those of the individual. They call us to make them a reality under our present historical conditions.

Beginning with the historical-critical work of Rudolf Bultmann these writers elaborate on his method of demythologizing or translating the message of the New Testament out of the mythical language in which it was handed down into a language intelligible in our lives. In Bultmann's perspective one always begins with the preunderstanding one brings to the text concerning the meaning of existence. For this reason interpretation is a *hermeneutical circle.* It is influenced by the preunderstanding of the one asking the questions, yet the process of demythologizing can be a tool for seeking to understand the mythical thought world in which New Testament stories were recorded and interpreting them into the scientific thought world of contemporary society.[27]

In developing a sociocritical hermeneutical circle the writers make use of the historical-critical method and the idea of the hermeneutical circle within which we operate, and then they seek to elaborate ways to be more self-critical of one's own preunderstandings, and of contemporary views of reality into which we translate the message. An example of this development may be seen in Segundo's *The Liberation of Theology*. The method he seeks to develop in liberating theology to serve the oppressed people of the world instead of the dominant groups of society is that of "the hermeneutic circle."[28]

The eschatological hermeneutic being used in this discussion of the future of partnership contains many of the same elements as those used by Segundo: the realization that there is no way to step outside of the circle to attain complete "objectivity"; the critical questioning based on one's own experience of reality; and the attempt to act out the interpretation in social and not just individual life. Yet in my opinion, the eschatological message does not allow us to tie our method of interpretation so closely to any one political commitment. That we must make particular political commitments and risk acting upon them seems to me to be very clear. But that this commitment should have such weight in interpreting the meaning of the Biblical text seems to ignore the integrity of the message itself which, through the action of God's Spirit, has power to work through many means of interpretation in opening up future and hope.

Eschatological hermeneutic is a process of questioning our actions and our society in the light of the eschatological message of the Bible. We begin with the *questions* that arise out of our life and out of the experience of those who cry out for deliverance; not simply with those of the "non-believer" but with those of the "non-person."[29] These questions are addressed critically to the tradition of the Christian faith and to the Bible as the chief witness to God's promise in Jesus Christ. The *Biblical message*, in turn, helps us to interpret itself, for a central motif of the Bible, according to Walter Harrelson, is that of "promise on the way to fulfillment."[30] In the light of the moving horizon of God's promise for New Creation one interprets the texts, knowing that full eschatological verification of one's interpretation can come only in the fulfillment of the New Creation.

The Coming One is already present with us as we live out his story. It is *living out that story* in order to give an account of the hope that is in us that helps us to discover the meaning of that story **even** as we continue our life in the Old Creation (I Peter 3:15–16). Having lived out the story and our questions addressed to it, we may discover clues out of tradition that may guide us as we seek to live now, as if we were part of God's New Creation. The *clues about God's action* are likely to be consistent with the way God has acted in the past in handing over Jesus Christ into the hands of all generations and nations (Rom. 8:31–32). The clues about the traditioning process in our own lives as the still living and evolving past by which we shape the future are likely to point us to new questions about areas in our own lives that matter for us as persons addressed by God to live out God's will on earth. Each new question sends us back to a critical analysis of our life and social reality and back to the eschatological message of the Bible, for the hermeneutic itself is an ongoing process and our answers are always provisional.

Life in the New Creation is one that is lived now, in the midst of the world "as if (we did it) not" *(hōs mē)*. In order to understand how this life of Christian freedom is carried out, let us look at the meaning of the words *hōs mē* as used by Paul in Bultmann's translation of I Cor. 7:29–31:

> let those who have wives be as if they had not,
> and those who mourn as if they mourned not,
> and those who rejoice as if they rejoiced not,
> and those who buy as if they possessed not,
> and those who have to do with the world as if they
> had nothing to do with it.[31]

The thrust of this passage is not simply that of a "dialectic of worldliness and unworldliness and, therefore, of eschatological tension," as Karl Barth maintains in his debate with Bultmann over the nature of Christian existence.[32] If it were simply that, we would concur with Barth that it is not an adequate description of the calling of the Christian to service and witness to God's action in the world. But there is more than that implied in Paul's use of *hōs mē*.

Looking at the text of I Corinthians 7, we notice that Paul's extensive teaching on the problems of marriage and celibacy is a piece of his own eschatological hermeneutics. In the light of the end which is breaking in, it is better to live *as if* the New Age is already here. In apocalyptic categories such a life would be one lived in the face of "the impending distress" (I Cor. 7:26). In adventology, which interprets the future as the *new* breaking into history now, emphasis would be on the fact of God's continued action in opening the future that sets us free to live in the Old Creation, as if we were part of the New Creation.

According to Paul, living *as if* we are in God's New Age leads us to live *as if not* in regard to the customs and relationships considered of ultimate importance in this age (Rom. 14:14). This is not simply because the time is short so *nothing really matters*. It is because there is *something that really matters*.[33] What really matters is the gift of God's love for humanity and the commission to proclaim the good news of that love. Because God's love is a "free gift" in Jesus Christ and nothing can separate us from that love, the patterns of our relationships, our occupations and preoccupations in this world are not of ultimate importance (Phil. 3:7).[34] The gift is for everyone and it is of utmost significance that the message of God's promised liberation be shared with all (I Cor. 9:19). Without taking ourselves or our roles and status with ultimate importance, we are set free from ourselves, free to risk living out the promised partnership with our neighbors and with God. Yet taking that promise seriously, we are commissioned to work and pray that the liberation of all might be a reality now.

Perhaps such an understanding of *hōs mē* implied in the gift of grace and the commission to live out the gospel message in the world will help avoid some of the one-sided interpretations of I Corinthians 7. For some, New Creation becomes an excuse for ignoring the commission to participate with God in transforming the Old Creation, and thus leads to quietism or lack of action. For others, the idea that one can live as a Christian in whatever situation one is placed leads to ignoring the need to change the situation when it is oppressive or destructive so that it may become a sign of the New Age. For other interpreters the idea that one's sexuality is not of ultimate importance for the Christian in relation to God's promise leads to the idea that sexuality is to be excluded from discussions of the meaning of faithfulness. For myself, our relationship to Jesus Christ is of ultimate importance and all other things are *hōs mē* (I Cor. 7:39; Rom. 14:8). They are very important in working out the meaning of our stewardship of God's commission to work toward New Creation, but in themselves they do not avail to our salvation or liberation, and must be interpreted in the light of God's intended future.

Theological perspectives on the future present us with many challenges to discover the relationship of hoping and planning in the fact of a critical awareness of the present social contradictions of justice and wholeness. In our discussion of partnership with God and with others we can see that the nature of our hope is the key to our projects and plans. Our hope is in God who is the giver of good. Hearing the promise that we do not yet see, we continue to journey toward the One who offers the gift of new wholeness and life.

A key to our understanding of partnership is hope, for we hope in God and in others.[35] We have no guarantee, simply an expectation of faithfulness and love. We may have different plans and goals to realize, but it is a common hope in the One who is our future that provides a basis for a new focus of relationship in Jesus Christ.

> For I know the plans I have for you, says the LORD, plans for *shalom* and not for evil, to give you a future and a hope. (Jer. 29:11)

NOTES

Prologue

1. *Sexism in the 1970's—Discrimination Against Women* (Geneva: World Council of Churches, 1974); *Risk,* Vol. X, No. 2 (1974); "The Community of Women and Men in the Church: A Proposal for Study Groups," *The Ecumenical Review,* Vol. XXVII, No. 4 (Oct. 1975), reprint, pp. 1–8.

2. *Pro Mundi Vita Bulletin,* Vol. LIX (March 1976), pp. 4–10.

3. Letty M. Russell, *Human Liberation in a Feminist Perspective—A Theology* (The Westminster Press, 1974), p. 183.

4. Letty M. Russell (ed.), *The Liberating Word: A Guide to Nonsexist Interpretation of the Bible* (The Westminster Press, 1976), Ch. 4, "Changing Language and the Church," pp. 82–98.

5. Letty M. Russell, *Christian Education in Mission* (The Westminster Press, 1967).

6. Joan Arnold, United Theological Seminary, October 1975.

7. Unless otherwise indicated, all Bible quotations are from the *Revised Standard Version of the Holy Bible,* copyright 1946, 1952, 1971, 1973. Brackets indicate that I have substituted a word or phrase.

8. Maureen Wallin, Yale Divinity School, May 1978.

Introduction

1. *Webster's New Twentieth Century Dictionary,* rev. and ed. by Jean L. McKechnie (The World Publishing Company, 1974, Unabridged, Second Edition).

2. Max Warren, *Partnership: The Study of an Idea* (London: SCM Press, Ltd., 1965), pp. 13–14.

3. This list was compiled out of discussions of a class on "The Future of Partnership," at Pacific School of Religion, July 1977.

4. R. Buckminster Fuller, "Technology and the Human Environ-

ment," in Alvin Toffler (ed.), *The Futurists* (Random House, Inc., 1972), p. 300; Daniel Bell, "The Year 2000—Trajectory of an Idea," *Daedalus,* Vol. 96, No. 3 (Summer 1967), pp. 650–651. According to *Webster's New Twentieth Century Dictionary,* serendipity is "an apparent aptitude for making fortunate discoveries accidentally."

5. Gerhard Kittel (ed.), *Theological Dictionary of the New Testament,* tr. and ed. by Geoffrey W. Bromiley (Wm. B. Eerdmans Publishing Company, 1965), Vol. II, p. 831.

6. Warren, *Partnership,* pp. 52–53.

PART I. PARTNERSHIP WITH GOD

1. Isa. 43:18–21. Translation from Letty M. Russell, *Ferment of Freedom* (National Board, YWCA, 600 Lexington Avenue, New York, N.Y. 10022, 1972), p. 85.

1. GOD'S ARITHMETIC

1. Gordon D. Kaufman, *God the Problem* (Harvard University Press, 1972), pp. 140–147.

2. Jürgen Moltmann, "Theology as Eschatology," in Frederick Herzog (ed.), *The Future of Hope: Theology as Eschatology* (Herder & Herder, Inc., 1970), pp. 8–11.

3. Oscar Cullmann, "Eschatology and Missions in the New Testament," in Gerald H. Anderson (ed.), *The Theology of the Christian Mission* (McGraw-Hill Book Co. Inc., 1961), p. 46.

4. Oscar Cullmann, *Salvation in History,* tr. by Sidney G. Sowers (Harper & Row, Publishers, Inc., 1967), p. 25; cf. Reginald H. Fuller, "Some Further Reflections on Heilsgeschichte," *Union Seminary Quarterly Review,* Vol. XXII, No. 2 (Jan. 1967), pp. 93–103; Gerhard von Rad, *Old Testament Theology,* tr. by D. M. G. Stalker (Harper & Row, Publishers, Inc., 1965), Vol. II, p. 44.

5. Thomas F. Torrance, "The Implications of *Oikonomia* for Knowledge and Speech of God in Early Christian Theology," in Felix Christ (ed.), *Ökonomia: Heilsgeschichte als Thema der Theologie* (Hamburg-Bergstedt: Herbert Reich Evang. Verlag, 1967), p. 226.

6. Gerhard Ebeling, "Theologie, I. Begriffs-Geschichtlich," *Die Religion in Geschichte und Gegenwart* (Tübingen: J. C. B. Mohr, 1962), VI, 7578.

7. M. D. Chenu, "The History of Salvation and the Historicity of Man in the Renewal of Theology," in L. K. Shook (ed.), *Theology of Renewal* (Herder & Herder, Inc., 1968), pp. 155–156.

8. Moltmann, "Theology as Eschatology," in Herzog (ed.), *The Future of Hope,* p. 8.

9. Karl Barth, *Church Dogmatics,* Vol. I, Pt. 1, tr. by G. T. Thomson (Edinburgh: T. & T. Clark, 1936); Karl Rahner, *The Trinity,* tr. by Joseph Donceel (Herder & Herder, Inc., 1970).

10. Karl Rahner, *Theological Investigations,* Vol. IV, tr. by Kevin Smith (The Seabury Press, Inc., 1974), p. 99; Karl Rahner, "Trinity, Divine," in Karl Rahner *et al.* (eds.), *Sacramentum Mundi* (Herder & Herder, Inc., 1970), Vol. VI, pp. 295–303.

11. Jürgen Moltmann, *The Crucified God,* tr. by R. A. Wilson and John Bowden (Harper & Row, Publishers, Inc., 1974), p. 238.

12. José Miguez-Bonino, *Doing Theology in a Revolutionary Situation* (Fortress Press, 1975), p. 145; Gustavo Gutiérrez, *A Theology of Liberation,* tr. and ed. by Caridad Inda and John Eagleson (Orbis Books, 1973), p. 265; James H. Cone, *God of the Oppressed* (The Seabury Press, Inc., 1975), pp. 138–141.

13. Paul H. Santmire, "Retranslating 'Our Father': The Urgency and the Possibility," *Dialog,* Vol. XVI (Spring 1977), pp. 101–106; Carol Ochs, *Behind the Sex of God* (Beacon Press, Inc., 1977), pp. 120, 129.

14. Rahner, "Trinity, Divine," in Rahner *et al.* (eds.), *Sacramentum Mundi,* Vol. VI, p. 298.

15. Margaret Farley, "New Patterns of Relationship: Beginnings of a Moral Revolution," *Theological Studies,* Vol. XXXVI, No. 4 (Dec. 1975), p. 642.

16. Rahner, *Theological Investigations,* Vol. IV, p. 94.

17. Moltmann, *The Crucified God,* p. 241.

18. George H. Tavard, "Sexist Language in Theology," *Theological Studies,* Vol. 36, No. 4 (Dec. 1975), p. 717.

19. Hans Conzelmann, *An Outline of the Theology of the New Testament,* tr. by John Bowden (Harper & Row, Publishers, Inc., 1969), pp. 99–106.

20. Stanley Marrow, "God the Father in the New Testament," Working Paper for the Boston Area, World Council of Churches' Task Force on Women and Men in the Church (Andover Newton Theological School, March 27, 1975).

21. Santmire, "Retranslating 'Our Father,' " p. 105.

22. Russell (ed.), *The Liberating Word,* pp. 88–94; Jay Williams, "Yahweh, Women and the Trinity," *Theology Today,* Vol. XXXII, No. 3 (Oct. 1975), pp. 238–240; Phyllis Trible, "God, Nature of, in the O.T.," *The Interpreter's Dictionary of the Bible,* Supplementary Volume (Abingdon Press, 1976), p. 368.

23. Farley, "New Patterns," p. 642.

24. *Ibid.,* p. 643.

25. Russell, *Human Liberation,* pp. 102–103.

26. "I Wish I Knew How It Would Feel to Be Free," by Billy Taylor

and Dick Dallas (copyright 1964 by Duane Music, Inc., 119 W. 57th Street, New York, N.Y. 10019).

27. Kittel (ed.), *Theological Dictionary of the New Testament,* Vol. V, pp. 801–802.

28. Diane Jagdeo, Yale Divinity School, in a class on "Issues in Liberation Theology," November 1977.

29. *The New English Bible* (Oxford University Press and Cambridge University Press, 1970).

30. Hans-Ruedi Weber, "God's Arithmetic," in Gerald H. Anderson and Thomas F. Stransky (eds.), *Mission Trends, No. 2: Evangelization* (Paulist Press, 1975), p. 65.

31. *Ibid.,* p. 66.

32. Letty M. Russell, "Women: Education Through Participation," *Religious Education,* Vol. LXX, No. 1 (Jan.-Feb. 1975), pp. 45–53.

33. Paul K. Jewett, *Man as Male and Female* (Wm. B. Eerdmans Publishing Company, 1975), pp. 33–34, 41.

34. Christopher Mwoleka, "Trinity and Community," in Gerald H. Anderson and Thomas F. Stransky (eds.), *Mission Trends, No. 3: Third World Theologies* (Paulist Press, 1976), p. 151; cf. "Uhuru na Ujamaa," *Risk,* Vol. VIII, No. 1 (1972), pp. 29–33; A. Falinjuma, "The Political System in Tanzania," *Risk,* Vol. X, No. 4 (1974), pp. 10–12.

35. Patricia Washburn, "The Return of the Gleaners," *The Christian Century,* Vol. XCV, No. 21 (June 7-14, 1978), pp. 622–624.

2. GOD'S UTOPIA

1. Letty M. Russell, "The Freedom of God," *Enquiry,* Vol. 8, No. 1 (Sept.-Nov. 1975), pp. 27–48.

2. Herzog (ed.), *The Future of Hope,* p. 34.

3. Hans Küng, *On Being a Christian,* tr. by E. Quinn (Doubleday & Company, Inc., 1976), p. 224; cf. Johannes B. Metz, *Theology of the World,* tr. by William Glen-Doepel (Herder & Herder, Inc., 1969), p. 88.

4. Herzog (ed.), *The Future of Hope,* p. 29.

5. Oscar Cullmann, *The Christology of the New Testament,* tr. by Shirley C. Guthrie and Charles A. M. Hall (The Westminster Press, 1959), pp. 170–171.

6. Dietrich Bonhoeffer, *Creation and Fall* (The Macmillan Company, 1959), p. 62.

7. Katherine D. Sakenfeld, "The Bible and Women: Bane or Blessing?" *Theology Today,* Vol. XXXII, No. 3 (Oct. 1975), p. 224. Cf. P. A. H. DeBoer, *Fatherhood and Motherhood in Israelite and Judean Piety* (Leiden: E. J. Brill, 1974), pp. 46–48.

8. Sakenfeld, "The Bible and Women," p. 225.

9. *Ibid.,* pp. 225–226.

10. Bonhoeffer, *Creation and Fall,* p. 37; cf. also Barth, *Church Dogmatics,* Vol. II, Pt. 1 (1957), p. 254; Vol. III, Pt. 2 (1960), pp. 261ff.

11. Gordon D. Kaufman, *Systematic Theology: A Historicist Perspective* (Charles Scribner's Sons, 1968), p. 330.

12. Diane Jagdeo, "A Theology of the Neighbor," unpublished STM thesis, Yale Divinity School, 1978; cf. Margaret Mead, "Cultural Man," in Egbert de Vries (ed.), *Man in Community* (Association Press, 1966), p. 209.

13. *Webster's New International Dictionary of the English Language,* 2d ed., unabridged, William Neilson, ed. in chief (G. & C. Merriam Company, 1954).

14. David Roberts, *Existentialism and Religious Belief,* ed. by Roger Hazelton (Oxford University Press, 1959), p. 296.

15. Dietrich Bonhoeffer, *Letters and Papers from Prison,* ed. by Eberhard Bethge and tr. by Reginald H. Fuller (The Macmillan Company, 1953), p. 179.

16. Paul Lehmann, *Ethics in a Christian Context* (Harper & Row, Publishers, Inc., 1963), pp. 117–123.

17. Jewett, *Man as Male and Female,* p. 23.

18. Emil Brunner, *Man in Revolt* (The Westminster Press, 1957), p. 345; Barth, *Church Dogmatics,* Vol. III, Pt. 4 (1961), p. 117.

19. Carolyn G. Heilbrun, *Toward a Recognition of Androgyny* (Harper & Row, Publishers, Inc., 1973), pp. ix–x; Eugene Bianchi, "Psychic Celibacy and the Quest for Mutuality," in Rosemary Ruether and Eugene Bianchi, *From Machismo to Mutuality: Man-Woman Liberation in America* (Paulist Press, 1976), p. 91.

20. Rosemary Radford Ruether, *New Woman, New Earth: Sexist Ideologies and Human Liberation* (The Seabury Press, Inc., 1975), p. 6.

21. Ann Belford Ulanov, "C. G. Jung on Male and Female," in Ruth Barnhouse and Urban Holmes III (eds.), *Male and Female: Christian Approaches to Sexuality* (The Seabury Press, Inc., 1976), pp. 197–210.

22. Barth, *Church Dogmatics,* Vol. III, Pt. 4, pp. 168–169.

23. Jewett, *Man as Male and Female,* pp. 29–30.

24. Sheila Collins, *A Different Heaven and Earth* (Judson Press, 1974); Ruether, *New Woman, New Earth.*

25. Kittel (ed.), *Theological Dictionary of the New Testament,* Vol. II, pp. 830–832.

26. Robin A. Scroggs, "Paul and the Eschatological Woman," *Journal of the American Academy of Religion,* Vol. XL (1972), pp. 285–287.

27. Kittel, *Theological Dictionary of the New Testament,* Vol. III, pp. 804–809.

28. Here I am indebted to the questions about the meaning of "clues"

raised by my class on "Partnership in Eschatological Perspective," Yale Divinity School, Spring 1978.

29. Janet Saltzman Chafetz, *Masculine/Feminine or Human?: An Overview of the Sociology of Sex Roles* (F. E. Peacock Publishers, Inc., 1974), p. 165.

30. *Ibid.,* p. 158.

31. Ernst Käsemann, *Essays on New Testament Times* (London: SCM Press, Ltd., 1964), p. 70.

32. Elias Andrews, "Spiritual Gifts," in George A. Buttrick *et al.* (eds.), *The Interpreter's Dictionary of the Bible (IDB),* Vol. IV (Abingdon Press, 1962), p. 435.

33. Dallas Lee, *The Cotton Patch Evidence: The Story of Clarence Jordan and the Koinonia Farm Experiment* (Harper & Row, Publishers, Inc., 1971).

34. *Ibid.,* p. 205; quoted by Howard W. Lull, "Koinonia Updated," *The Christian Century,* Vol. XCIII, No. 32 (Oct. 13, 1976), p. 869.

35. Lull, "Koinonia Updated," p. 870.

36. Letha Scanzoni and Nancy Hardesty, *All We're Meant to Be: A Biblical Approach to Women's Liberation* (Word, Inc., 1974), p. 87.

37. Robin Morgan, *Going Too Far: The Personal Chronicle of a Feminist* (Random House, Inc., 1977), pp. 8–9.

3. GOD'S SELF-PRESENTATION

1. Russell, *Human Liberation,* pp. 135–140.

2. Dorothee Soelle, *Christ the Representative* (Fortress Press, 1967), p. 15.

3. Report of the New York Study on "Community of Women and Men in the Church," Commission of Faith and Order, National Council of the Churches of Christ, Minutes of the meeting of June 4, 1975, New York, p. 2; cf. Mary Daly, *Beyond God the Father: Toward a Philosophy of Women's Liberation* (Beacon Press, Inc., 1973), pp. 19–23; Collins, *A Different Heaven and Earth,* pp. 217–218.

4. Bernhard W. Anderson, "Lord," *IDB,* Vol. III, pp. 150–151.

5. Trible, "God, Nature of, in the O.T.," *IDB,* Sup. Vol., pp. 368–369.

6. Paul D. Hanson, "Masculine Metaphors for God and Sex Discrimination in the Old Testament," *The Ecumenical Review,* Vol. XXVII, No. 4 (Oct. 1975), pp. 316, 323.

7. *Ibid.,* p. 323.

8. Cullmann, *Christology,* pp. 78–79.

9. *Ibid.,* pp. 160–161; cf. Norman Perrin, "Son of Man," *IDB,* Sup. Vol., pp. 833–836.

10. Perrin, "Son of Man," IDB, Sup. Vol., p. 835.

11. Cullmann, *Christology,* p. 181.

12. Cone, *God of the Oppressed,* p. 75.

13. Howard Yoder, *The Politics of Jesus* (Wm. B. Eerdmans Publishing Company, 1972), pp. 163–192.

14. Hans Hoekendijk, *Horizons of Hope* (Tidings, 1970), p. 30.

15. Beverly Harrison, "Some Ethical Issues in the Women's Movement." Unpublished paper delivered at the American Society of Christian Ethics, Jan. 18, 1974 (mimeographed), p. 4.

16. Jean Baker Miller, *Toward a New Psychology of Women* (Beacon Press, Inc., 1976), p. 71.

17. Jean Stapleton and Richard Bright, *Equal Marriage* (Abingdon Press, 1976), pp. 13–21.

18. Miller, *Toward a New Psychology of Women,* p. 72.

19. *Ibid.,* pp. 29–35.

20. Paulo Freire, *Pedagogy of the Oppressed* (Herder & Herder, Inc., 1970); cf. Paul Tillich, *Love, Power and Justice* (Oxford University Press, 1954), p. 40.

21. Miller, *Toward a New Psychology of Women,* p. 125.

22. Ruether, *New Woman, New Earth,* p. 66.

23. Martin Luther, "A Treatise on Christian Liberty (1520)," *Works of Martin Luther,* Vol. II, tr. by A. T. W. Steinhaeuser (Muhlenberg Press, 1943, the Philadelphia Edition), p. 312.

24. Hoekendijk, *Horizons of Hope,* p. 33.

25. Küng, *On Being a Christian,* p. 282.

26. Elizabeth Carroll, "Women and Ministry," *Theological Studies,* Vol. 36, No. 4 (Dec. 1975), p. 683; cf. also Raymond Brown, "Women in the Fourth Gospel," *ibid.,* p. 690.

27. Margaret Farley, "Moral Imperatives for the Ordination of Women," in Anne Marie Gardiner (ed.), *Women and Catholic Priesthood: An Expanded Vision* (Paulist Press, 1976), p. 39.

28. James Ramey, *Intimate Friendships* (Prentice-Hall, Inc., 1976), p. 44.

29. Käsemann, *Essays on New Testament Times,* p. 76.

30. Richard D. N. Dickinson (ed.), *To Set at Liberty the Oppressed: Toward an Understanding of Christian Responsibilities for Development and Liberation* (Geneva: World Council of Churches, 1975), p. 68.

31. Emmanuel McCall, "Partners in Liberation: The Black Church and Social Justice," *Partners in Ministry* (Atlanta: Southern Baptist Home Mission Board, 1977), pp. 8–11.

32. Sandol Stoddard, *The Hospice Movement: A Better Way of Caring for the Dying* (Stein & Day, 1977). Cf. Donald J. Gaetz, "A Covenant Until Death," *New World Outlook,* Vol. LXVIII, No. 6 (June 1978), pp. 20–23.

33. Elizabeth O'Connor, *The New Community* (Harper & Row, Publishers, Inc., 1976), pp. 24–56.

34. Freire, *Pedagogy of the Oppressed,* p. 162; cf. "The Militant Observer: A Sociological Alternative" (Geneva: Institute of Cultural Action, 1975); Faye Aaker, "The Stimulator Sociologist: A Case Study," unpublished M.A. dissertation, University of Miami, 1978.

35. John Booth Brock, "What Feminist Liberation Means to Me," unpublished term paper, Yale Divinity School, Jan. 5, 1978.

4. ESCHATOLOGY AND SEXUALITY

1. See "Image of God" in Chapter 2.

2. Anthony Kosnik *et al., Human Sexuality: New Directions in American Catholic Thought,* A Study Commissioned by the Catholic Theological Society of America (Paulist Press, 1977), p. 29. Cited hereafter as *Catholic Theological Report.*

3. See "Clues from God's Arithmetic" in Chapter 1.

4. Tom E. Driver, "Human Sexuality," *Christianity and Crisis,* Vol. XXXVII, No. 17 (Oct. 31, 1977), p. 246. See Chapter 8, "Partnership and the Future."

5. *Catholic Theological Report,* p. 86.

6. *Ibid.,* p. 82.

7. Norman Pittenger, "A Theological Approach to Homosexuality," in Barnhouse and Holmes (eds.), *Male and Female,* p. 161.

8. "Sexuality and the Church," *JSAC Grapevine,* Vol. V, No. 1 (June 1973), p. 2.

9. Ruether and Bianchi, *From Machismo to Mutuality,* p. 75.

10. "A Progress Report to the 'Theology in the Americas' Group," Boston Industrial Mission, Cambridge, Mass., April 1976 (mimeographed).

11. *JSAC Grapevine,* Vol. V, No. 1 (June 1973), p. 1. The distinction was first suggested by SIECUS (Sex Information and Education Council of the United States).

12. *Human Sexuality: A Preliminary Study* by the United Church of Christ (United Church Press, 1977), p. 13. Cited hereafter as *UCC Report.*

13. Audrey Lorde, "Scratching the Surface: Some Notes on Barriers to Women Loving," *Black Scholar,* Vol. IX, No. 7 (April 1978), p. 31.

14. "Report of the Task Force to Study Homosexuality," Blue Book I, General Assembly of The United Presbyterian Church U.S.A., 1978. Cited hereafter as *UPCUSA Report.* Cf. John Money and Patricia Tucker, *Sexual Signatures: On Being a Man or a Woman* (Little, Brown & Company, 1975), pp. 36–62.

15. *UPCUSA Report,* pp. 11–12.

16. Chafetz, *Masculine/Feminine or Human?,* p. 3.

17. Letha Scanzoni and Virginia R. Mollenkott, *Is the Homosexual*

My Neighbor? (Harper & Row, Publishers, Inc., 1978), p. 93.

18. *Ibid.*, pp. 18–20. Cf. Alfred C. Kinsey *et al., Sexual Behavior in the Human Male* (W. B. Saunders Company, 1948); Alfred C. Kinsey *et al., Sexual Behavior in the Human Female* (W. B. Saunders Company, 1953); Robert J. Stroller, "The 'Bedrock' of Masculinity and Femininity: Bisexuality," in Jean Baker Miller (ed.), *Psychoanalysis and Women* (Brunner/Mazel, Inc., 1973), pp. 245–254.

19. *UCC Report,* pp. 134–136.

20. *UCC Report; Catholic Theological Report;* cf. also Donald Goergen, *The Sexual Celibate* (The Seabury Press, Inc., 1974), pp. 13–88; cf. Scanzoni and Mollenkott, *Is the Homosexual My Neighbor?,* pp. 54–72.

21. Trible, "God, Nature of, in the O.T.," *IDB,* Sup. Vol., p. 368.

22. *Ibid.*

23. Walter Brueggemann, "Israel's Social Criticism and Yahweh's Sexuality," *Journal of the American Academy of Religion,* Vol. XLV, No. 3 Supplement (Sept. 1977), pp. 759–761.

24. Samuel Terrien, "Toward a Biblical Theology of Womanhood," *Religion in Life,* Autumn 1973, p. 329.

25. *Catholic Theological Report,* p. 7.

26. John McNeill, *The Church and the Homosexual* (Sheed, Andrews & McMeel, Inc., 1976), p. 60.

27. James B. Nelson, "Homosexuality and the Church," *Christianity and Crisis,* Vol. XXXVII, No. 5 (April 4, 1977), p. 64; *Catholic Theological Report,* p. 15.

28. McNeill, *The Church and the Homosexual,* p. 66.

29. See "Theological Perspectives on the Future" in Chapter 8.

30. Margaret Farley, "Issues in Sexual Ethics," unpublished speech at "Tomorrow in August," a meeting of the Province of Detroit Sisters of Mercy, Aug. 13, 1976.

31. Cf. *Daedalus,* Vol. CVI, No. 2 (Spring 1977), issue on "The Family"; *Black Scholar,* Vol. IX, No. 7 (April 1978), issue on "Blacks and Sexual Revolution."

32. *UCC Report,* p. 23. Quoted from Marvin B. Sussman, "Family Sociology," in Margaret S. Archer (ed.), *Current Research in Sociology* (The Hague: Mouton, 1974).

33. *UCC Report,* pp. 22–23.

34. Gibson Winter, "Women's Liberation: The Culture Context," *Theology Today,* Vol. XXXIV, No. 4 (Jan. 1978), pp. 411–413.

35. Elizabeth F. Hood, "Black Women, White Women: Separate Paths to Liberation," *Black Scholar* (April 1978), p. 54.

36. Women's Bureau, U.S. Department of Labor, Washington, D.C.

37. Caryl Rivers, "Egalitarian Marriage: No More Ring Around the Collar," *Mother Jones,* Vol. II, No. 9 (Nov. 1977), pp. 39–48.

38. Ruether and Bianchi, *From Machismo to Mutuality;* Glenn R. Bucher (ed.), *Straight/White/Male* (Fortress Press, 1976); Joseph H. Pleck and Jack Sawyer (eds.), *Men and Masculinity* (Prentice-Hall, Inc., 1974).

39. Ross Wetzsteon, "The Feminist Man?," *Mother Jones,* Vol. II, No. 9 (Nov. 1977), pp. 52–59.

40. Michelle Zimbalist Rosaldo and Louise Lamphere (eds.), *Woman, Culture, and Society* (Stanford University Press, 1974).

41. *UCC Report,* pp. 24–28.

42. James Ramey, "Multi-Adult Household: Living Group of the Future?" *The Futurist,* April 1976, pp. 78–83.

43. Ramey, *Intimate Friendships,* pp. 17–24; cf. Marcia Seligson, *Options: A Personal Expedition Through the Sexual Frontier* (Random House, Inc., 1978).

44. McNeill, *The Church and the Homosexual,* pp. 40–41.

45. *UCC Report,* pp. 172–173; cf. Robert Dow, *Ministry with Single Adults* (Judson Press, 1977).

46. Ramey, *Intimate Friendships,* pp. 17–24.

47. *UCC Report,* p. 23. See note 33, above.

48. *Ibid.,* p. 190; cf. Wolfgang Roth and Rosemary Radford Ruether, *The Liberating Bond: Covenants—Biblical and Contemporary* (Friendship Press, 1978), pp. 54–59.

49. Daniel Day Williams, *The Spirit and the Forms of Love* (Harper & Row, Publishers, Inc., 1968), p. 220.

50. Cf. "Theological Perspectives on the Future" in Chapter 8.

51. Ruether and Bianchi, *From Machismo to Mutuality,* p. 135.

52. *Catholic Theological Report,* p. 83.

53. Driver, "Human Sexuality," p. 246.

54. Tom F. Driver, "Sexuality and Jesus," in Martin E. Marty and Dean G. Peerman (eds.), *New Theology* No. 3 (The Macmillan Company, 1966), p. 131; cf. Rosemary Ruether, "What Do the Synoptics Say? The Sexuality of Jesus," *Christianity and Crisis,* Vol. XXXVIII, No. 8 (May 29, 1978), pp. 134–137.

5. ADVENT SHOCK AND THE CHURCH

1. See Chapter 8, "Partnership and the Future."

2. J. C. Hoekendijk, *The Church Inside Out,* ed. by L. A. Hoedemaker and Pieter Tijmes and tr. by Isaac C. Rottenberg (The Westminster Press, 1966), p. 181.

3. Ruether and Bianchi, *From Machismo to Mutuality,* p. 135.

4. Alvin Toffler, *Future Shock* (Bantam Books, Inc., 1970), pp. 10–12.

5. Victor Ferkiss, *Technological Man* (Mentor Books, 1969), p. 25.

6. Russell, *Ferment of Freedom,* p. 188.

7. Hoekendijk, *The Church Inside Out,* pp. 171–189.

8. See "Clues from God's Utopia" in Chapter 2.

9. Metz, *Theology of the World,* p. 94.

10. Patricia Budd Kepler, "Women Clergy and the Cultural Order," *Theology Today,* Vol. XXXIV, No. 4 (Jan. 1978), p. 403; Ann Douglas, *The Feminization of American Culture* (Alfred A. Knopf, Inc., 1977).

11. Winter, "Women's Liberation: The Culture Context," pp. 415–420.

12. Miller, *Toward a New Psychology of Women,* p. 29; see "Partnership and Hierarchy" in Chapter 3.

13. O'Connor, *The New Community,* pp. 100–117.

14. "Emerging Liberation Churches" (United Church Board of Homeland Ministries, 287 Park Avenue South, New York, N.Y. 10010).

15. Avery Dulles, *Models of the Church* (Doubleday & Company, Inc., 1974), pp. 83–96.

16. *Ibid.,* p. 86.

17. *Ibid.,* p. 93.

18. *Ibid.,* pp. 92–94; but cf. R. D. Haight, "Mission: The Symbol for Understanding the Church Today," in Walter J. Burghardt and William G. Thompson (eds.), *Why the Church?* (Paulist Press, 1976), pp. 76–107.

19. Paul S. Minear, *Images of the Church in the New Testament* (The Westminster Press, 1960), p. 66. Cf. also Norman Gottwald, *The Church Unbound* (J. B. Lippincott Company, 1967), for a discussion of the relation of church and culture and of Israel and the nations.

20. Minear, *Images,* pp. 223–224, 248.

21. *Ibid.,* p. 133.

22. *Ibid.,* pp. 67, 173ff.

23. John A. T. Robinson, *On Being the Church in the World* (The Westminster Press, 1962), p. 132.

24. James W. Jones, "The Practice of Peoplehood: The Call to Be a Servant Community," *Sojourners,* Vol. VI, No. 5 (May 1977), pp. 5–10.

25. Ernst Käsemann, *Jesus Means Freedom,* tr. by Frank Clarke (Fortress Press, 1969), p. 149.

26. Cone, *God of the Oppressed,* p. 234.

27. Arend Th. van Leeuwen, "Cultural Unity and Pluralism," de Vries (ed.), *Man in Community,* pp. 294–295.

28. Janice Harayda, "Alone in the Pew," *A.D.,* Vol. VII, No. 3 (March 1978), pp. 16–21; *UCC Report,* pp. 142–191.

29. Jim Comer, "Another View," *Network News,* Nov. 1977 (The Witherspoon Society, 236 W. 73d Street, New York, N.Y. 10023), p. 4.

30. Jürgen Moltmann, *Theology of Hope* (Harper & Row, Publishers, Inc., 1965), pp. 310–311.

31. Letty M. Russell, "Shalom in Postmodern Society," in John H. Westerhoff III (ed.), *A Colloquy on Christian Education* (United Church Press, 1972), pp. 98–99.

32. Memorial Service for Harold Eads, Church of the Ascension, 340 E. 106th Street, New York City, Dec. 22, 1977; "They Cast Their Nets in Galilee" by W. A. Percy, *Pilgrim Hymnal* (The Pilgrim Press, 1958), Hymn 340.

33. Russell, *Christian Education in Mission,* pp. 40–41; cf. *The Church for Others* (Geneva: World Council of Churches, 1967).

34. Dulles, *Models of the Church,* p. 93.

35. O'Connor, *The New Community,* p. 59.

36. Letty M. Russell, "Tradition as Mission: Study of a New Current in Theology and Its Implications for Theological Education," unpublished doctoral thesis, Union Theological Seminary, New York City, 1969, pp. 283–285.

37. *Ibid.,* pp. 54–56; Dulles, *Models of the Church,* p. 117.

38. Dom Helder Camâra, quoted from a speech at the International Eucharistic Congress in 1976 by Nancy E. Krody, "Woman, Lesbian, Feminist, Christian," *Christianity and Crisis,* Vol. XXXVII, Nos. 9 and 10 (May 30 and June 13, 1977), p. 136.

39. Jürgen Moltmann, "Hope in the Struggle of the People," *Christianity and Crisis,* Vol. XXXVII, No. 4 (March 21, 1977), p. 53.

40. Unpublished lecture by Hans Hoekendijk, Union Theological Seminary, New York City, Oct. 27, 1966.

41. Joseph Comblin, *The Meaning of Mission,* tr. by John Drury (Orbis Books, 1977), pp. 114–115.

42. Käsemann, *Essays on New Testament Times,* p. 65.

43. Russell, *Human Liberation,* pp. 31–33.

44. This pastor's name is unknown to me. He was doing doctoral work with Hans Hoekendijk in Utrecht.

45. Comblin, *The Meaning of Mission,* pp. 80–81.

46. Hans Hoekendijk, "The Church in Mission," address given at the Continental Missionary Consultation, Freudenstadt, October 1951 (mimeographed by the World Council of Churches), p. 10.

6. FLIGHT FROM MINISTRY

1. Otto Haendler, *Grundriss der praktischen Theologie* (Berlin: Alfred Töpelmann, 1957), p. 3.

2. *The Babylonian Captivity of the Church* (1520), *Works of Martin Luther,* Vol. II, p. 282.

3. For example, see Glenn Richard Bucher and Patricia Ruth Hill (eds.), *Confusion and Hope: Clergy, Laity, and the Church in Transition* (Fortress Press, 1974); Lewis S. Mudge (ed.), *Model for Ministry* (Philadelphia: Office of the General Assembly, The United Presbyterian Church U.S.A., 1970); H. Richard Niebuhr, *The Purpose of the Church and Its Ministry* (Harper & Brothers, 1956); Robert E. Terwilliger and Urban T. Holmes III (eds.), *To Be a Priest: Perspectives on Vocation and Ordination* (The Seabury Press, Inc., 1975); Gerald Moede, "A Survey of the Ecumenical Discussion Regarding Ordained Ministry in the 1970's" (Consultation on Church Union, 1977; mimeographed).

4. "Towards an Ecumenical Consensus on Baptism, Eucharist and Ministry," Report of the Faith and Order Standing Commission on the Churches' Replies to the Agreed Statements, "One Baptism, One Eucharist and a Mutually Recognized Ministry," July 18–24, 1977, Loccum, Federal Republic of Germany (Geneva: World Council of Churches, 1977). Cf. J. Lara-Braud, Jeanne Audrey Powers, "Ministry Shaped by Hope," paper for Consultation on Church Union for Task Force on Women, March 9–10, 1978 (mimeographed).

5. Russell, *Human Liberation,* p. 77.

6. Peter Lengsfeld, *Überlieferung* (Paderborn: Bonifacius-Druckerei, 1960), p. 23; Paul S. Minear (ed.), *Faith and Order Findings* (London: SCM Press, Ltd., 1963), "Tradition and Traditions," pp. 1–63; Oscar Cullmann, "The Tradition," *The Early Church,* ed. by A. J. B. Higgins (The Westminster Press, 1956), pp. 59–75.

7. V. L. Schmidt, *"Kaleō," "Klēsis,"* in Kittel (ed.), *Theological Dictionary of the New Testament,* Vol. III, pp. 487–493.

8. Gustaf Wingren, *Luther on Vocation* (Muhlenberg Press, 1957), pp. 1–4.

9. Russell, *Human Liberation,* p. 75.

10. This was pointed out in discussion and in a memo by Dr. John Bazeale at a meeting of the General Assembly Committee on Liberation and Renewal of The United Presbyterian Church U.S.A. in 1976. Cf. the Report of this Committee in the General Assembly *Minutes,* June 1977.

11. Ruether and Bianchi, *From Machismo to Mutuality,* p. 115.

12. Ruether, *New Woman, New Earth,* p. 75.

13. Daniel Day Williams, "Vocation in Christian Ministry," *Pastoral Psychology,* March 1961, pp. 8–12. Cf. also Bucher and Hill (eds.),

Confusion and Hope, pp. 32–47; Justus Freytag, "The Ministry as a Profession: A Sociological Critique," in David M. Paton (ed.), *New Forms of Ministry* (Edinburgh House Press, 1965), pp. 55–83.

14. Thomas F. Green, *Work, Leisure, and the American Schools* (Random House, Inc., 1968), pp. 76–92; Barbara Wilson, "A New Definition of 'Career,'" *Wellesley Alumnae Magazine,* Winter 1977, p. 33; Joseph Newman (ed.), *1994: The World of Tomorrow* (U.S. News & World Report, Inc., 1973), p. 171.

15. Report of the Program Agency to the 1975 General Assembly, The United Presbyterian Church U.S.A.

16. Cf. "A Partial Directory of Clergy Couples in Eight American Protestant Denominations," compiled by Nancy Jo Kemper von Lackum and John P. von Lackum, co-ministers, Pilgrim Congregational Church (United Church of Christ), 460 Lake Street, Oak Park, Ill. 60302 (mimeographed).

17. Donna Day-Laver, "Clergy Couples: Are They Working?" *Daughters of Sarah,* Vol. III, No. 2 (March 1977), pp. 1–3; John P. von Lackum and Nancy Jo Kemper von Lackum, "Collegial Ministry: Professional Partnership for Clergy Couples," and "Bed, Board, Babe and Bible: An Inside View of the Interpersonal Dynamics of Collegiality in Ministry and Marriage," Halford Luccock Lectures, Yale Divinity School, March 29–30, 1977 (mimeographed).

18. Mudge (ed.), *Model for Ministry,* pp. 32–34; Richard Nelson Bolles, *What Color Is Your Parachute? A Practical Manual for Job-Hunters and Career-Changers,* rev. ed. (Ten Speed Press, 1972), p. i; cf. interviews of seminary graduates not employed in the church by Edith O'Donnell, "Servants of Christ and Stewards of the Mysteries of God," Yale Divinity School, May 1976 (mimeographed).

19. Ivan Illich, "The Vanishing Clergyman," *The Critic,* Vol. XXV, No. 6 (June-July 1967), pp. 18–26; Joseph H. Fichter, "The Myth of the Hyphenated Clergy," *The Critic,* Vol. XXVIII, No. 3 (Dec. 1968–Jan. 1969), pp. 16–24.

20. David S. Schuller *et al., Readiness for Ministry,* 2 vols. (The Association of Theological Schools in the United States and Canada, Box 396, Vandalia, Ohio 45377; 1975, 1976); Kepler, "Women Clergy and the Cultural Order," p. 405.

21. G. Douglas Lewis (ed.), *Explorations in Ministry: A Report on the Ministry in the '70s Project* (IDOC-North America, 1971); *Ministry in Context: The Third Mandate Programme of the Theological Education Fund* (1970–77) (London: New Life Press, 1972).

22. *The Constitution of The United Presbyterian Church in the United States of America:* Part II, *Book of Order,* 1976–77, 82.04; O'Connor, *The New Community,* pp. 85–99.

23. C. H. Jacquet, "Women Ministers in 1977: A Report" (Office of

Research, Evaluation and Planning, National Council of Churches, March 1978), p. 13.

24. H. Richard Niebuhr and Daniel Day Williams (eds.), *The Ministry in Historical Perspective* (Harper & Brothers, 1956), pp. 19, 213; Hans Küng, *The Church,* tr. by Ray and Rosaleen Ockenden (Sheed & Ward, 1967), pp. 402–405.

25. Russell, *Human Liberation,* pp. 172–182.

26. *One Baptism, One Eucharist and a Mutually Recognized Ministry,* Faith and Order Paper No. 73 (Geneva: World Council of Churches, 1975), p. 33. Cf. also "Towards an Ecumenical Consensus on Baptism, Eucharist and Ministry," 1977. Cf. Moede, "A Survey," p. 18.

27. Cf. *Sojourners,* Vol. VI, No. 1 (January 1977), "A Portrait of Sojourners Fellowship," pp. 22–32.

28. Course on "The Future of Partnership," taught by Letty M. Russell, Summer 1977. Paper written by Mary Ellen Gaylord, Bill Hornbuckle, Marianna Kirwin, Martha Ward.

29. William John Best, "The Smallest Church with the Greatest Care," *A.D.,* Vol. VII, No. 6 (June/July 1978), pp. 41–43 (United Church of Christ edition).

7. LOVING THE QUESTIONS

1. Hoyt Hickman, *Ritual in a New Day: An Invitation* (Abingdon Press, 1976), pp. 73–127; Mudge (ed.), *Model for Ministry,* pp. 18–19, 33–34.

2. Rainer Maria Rilke, *Letters to a Young Poet,* rev. ed., tr. by M. D. Herter Norton (W. W. Norton & Company, Inc., 1954), p. 35.

3. Observation made by Elizabeth Thomsen, Pacific School of Religion, July 1977. The growth pattern of adults is explored in Gail Sheehy, *Passages* (Bantam Books, Inc., 1976).

4. Russell, *Christian Education in Mission,* p. 28; my partnership in learning and questioning is symbolized in this book by the notes referring to persons posing key questions for investigation.

5. Alvin Toffler, *Learning for Tomorrow* (Vintage Books, Inc., 1974); Jonathan Kozol, *The Night Is Dark and I Am Far from Home* (Houghton Mifflin Company, 1975); "Women in Theological Education: An Issue Reexamined," *Theological Education,* Vol. XI, No. 2 (Winter 1975).

6. Henri Nouwen, *Creative Ministry* (Doubleday & Company, Inc., 1971), pp. 2–20.

7. Ivan Illich, *Deschooling Society* (Harper & Row, Publishers, Inc., 1970), p. 17.

8. Freire, *Pedagogy of the Oppressed,* pp. 57ff.; cf. also *Risk,* Vol. VI,

No. 4 (1970), issue on "School or Scandal"; Paulo Freire, *Pedagogy in Process* (The Seabury Press, Inc., 1978).

9. Nouwen, *Creative Ministry,* pp. 4–9.

10. *Ibid.,* pp. 10–14.

11. *Ibid.,* p. 13.

12. Yale Divinity School, "Christian Witness in Contemporary Society," 1976–1977; 1977–1978.

13. Russell, *Christian Education in Mission,* p. 25.

14. Russell, "Tradition as Mission," p. 8.

15. Cf. the discussion of Greek words related to *oikos* in Chapter 1.

16. Russell, *Human Liberation,* p. 20.

17. C. Ellis Nelson, *Where Faith Begins* (John Knox Press, 1967); John H. Westerhoff III, *Will Our Children Have Faith?* (The Seabury Press, Inc., 1976).

18. *Enable,* May 1976 (The Christian Church of Northern California–Nevada, 111-A Fairmount Avenue, Oakland, Calif. 94611; mimeographed), p. 3.

19. *Work Book for the Fifth Assembly of the World Council of Churches* (Geneva: World Council of Churches, 1975), p. 40.

20. Freire, *Pedagogy of the Oppressed,* p. 19.

21. *Ibid.,* p. 66.

22. "Education, Liberation and Community," Dossier IV on the Sections of the Fifth Assembly, World Council of Churches (New York: World Council of Churches, 1974); cf. Charles Melchert, "The Future of Religious Education: Commitment in Religion and Education," in Gloria Durka and Joanmarie Smith (eds.), *Emerging Issues in Religious Education* (Paulist Press, 1976).

23. Margaret Mead, "The Future: Prefigurative Cultures and Unknown Children," reprinted in Toffler (ed.), *The Futurists,* pp. 27–50.

24. *Ibid.,* p. 27.

25. *Ibid.,* pp. 29–38; cf. also Chapter 6, "Flight from Ministry."

26. Mead, "The Future," in Toffler (ed.), *The Futurists,* p. 46.

27. Archibald MacLeish, quoted in *ibid.,* p. 48.

28. Robert Theobald, *An Alternative Future for America II* (Swallow Press, Inc., 1970), p. 77; cf. Illich, *Deschooling Society,* p. 17.

29. This was the experience of Bill Jacobs, Pacific School of Religion, Summer 1977.

30. Discussed in Theobald, *An Alternative Future,* pp. 160ff.

31. Freire, *Pedagogy of the Oppressed,* pp. 75–76.

32. Miller, *Toward a New Psychology of Women,* pp. 124–125.

33. Hans Hoekendijk, "Mission—A Celebration of Freedom," *Union Seminary Quarterly Review,* Vol. XXI, No. 2, Pt. 1 (Jan. 1966), pp. 141–143.

34. Paraphrase by Hans Hoekendijk and Letty Russell.

35. Hoekendijk, "Mission," p. 140.

36. Rilke, *Letters to a Young Poet,* p. 35; Robert H. Raines, *Living the Questions* (Word Books, 1977).

8. PARTNERSHIP AND THE FUTURE

1. David M. Paton (ed.), *Breaking Barriers: The Report of the Fifth Assembly of the World Council of Churches, Nairobi, 1975* (Wm. B. Eerdmans Publishing Company, 1976), pp. 3–37.

2. The phrasing of this question is from a response of Sr. Catherine Pinkerton in the mimeographed Working Papers for the International Colloquium on Women and Men as Partners in Christian Community, Louvain, Belgium, August 1975.

3. Eric Mount, *The Feminine Factor* (John Knox Press, 1973), p. 178.

4. Jürgen Moltmann, *Religion, Revolution, and the Future,* tr. by M. Douglas Meeks (Charles Scribner's Sons, 1969), p. 77.

5. Mead, "The Future: Prefigurative Cultures and Unknown Children," in Toffler (ed.), *The Futurists,* pp. 27–50.

6. Yujiro Hayashi, "The Information Centered Society," in Toffler (ed.), *The Futurists,* p. 245; cf. Willis W. Harman, *An Incomplete Guide to the Future* (San Francisco Book Company, Inc., 1976), pp. 28–37.

7. Chafetz, *Masculine/Feminine or Human?* p. 200; cf. also Glenn Bucher in "Liberation, Male and White: Initial Reflections," *The Christian Century,* Vol. XCI, No. 12 (March 20, 1974), p. 316, and Bucher (ed.), *Straight/White/Male.*

8. Ruether and Bianchi, *From Machismo to Mutuality.*

9. Ruether, *New Woman, New Earth,* p. xi; cf. also Jane Marie Lueke, "The Dominance Syndrome," *The Christian Century,* Vol. XCIV, No. 15 (April 27, 1977), pp. 405–407.

10. Miller, *Toward a New Psychology of Women,* p. 56. Cf. also Gail Sheehy, *Passages;* Doris Lessing, *The Summer Before the Dark* (Bantam Books, Inc., 1973); Carol Ochs, *Behind the Sex of God.*

11. Dorothee Soelle, "Meditation on Luke 1:46–55," in Clare B. Fischer *et al.* (eds.), *Women in a Strange Land: A Search for a New Image* (Fortress Press, 1975), pp. 79–80; Maricela Peraza and Harry Maurer, "Honduras: Did the Church Start Something It Can't Stop?" *Ms.,* Vol. VI, No. 2 (Aug. 1977), pp. 12–15; Margaret Mead, "Needed: Full Partnership for Women," *Saturday Review,* Vol. CCXII (June 14, 1975), pp. 26–27.

12. Farley, "New Patterns," p. 628.

13. The question that led me to this exploration was posed by Cyril Richardson at Union Theological Seminary, New York City, in 1975.

He asked me if there is a sufficient change going on in consciousness that it would warrant a new theology.

14. "The Future as Threat and Opportunity," in *The World Year Book of Religion: The Religious Situation* (Beacon Press, Inc., 1969), p. 925.

15. Miller, *Toward a New Psychology of Women*, p. 79.

16. William McNamara, "Christian Mysticism," lecture at Pacific School of Religion, July 12, 1977.

17. Moltmann, "Theology as Eschatology," in Herzog (ed.), *The Future of Hope*, p. 33; Metz, *Theology of the World*, p. 114.

18. Warren, *Partnership*, p. 11.

19. Juan Luis Segundo, *The Liberation of Theology* (Orbis Books, 1976).

20. Hoekendijk, *The Church Inside Out*, p. 23.

21. Ernst Käsemann, "On the Subject of Primitive Christian Apocalyptic," *New Testament Questions of Today*, tr. by W. J. Montague (Fortress Press, 1969), p. 137; Robin J. Scroggs, *Paul for a New Day* (Fortress Press, 1977), p. viii.

22. Russell (ed.), *The Liberating Word*, pp. 83–85.

23. Metz, *Theology of the World*, p. 112.

24. Dietrich Bonhoeffer, *Letters and Papers from Prison*, ed. by Eberhard Bethge, tr. by Reginald H. Fuller and rev. by Frank Clarke and others, 3d. English ed. (The Macmillan Company, 1967), p. 158. Quoted by Dorothee Soelle in *Political Theology*, tr. and intro. by John Shelley (Fortress Press, 1974), p. 1.

25. Metz, *Theology of the World;* Soelle, *Political Theology;* José Miranda, *Being and the Messiah*, tr. by John Eagleson (Orbis Books, 1977); Segundo, *The Liberation of Theology;* Miguez-Bonino, *Doing Theology in a Revolutionary Situation*.

26. Soelle, *Political Theology*, p. 15.

27. John Macquarrie, "Rudolf Bultmann," in Dean G. Peerman and Martin E. Marty (eds.), *A Handbook of Christian Theologians* (The World Publishing Company, 1965), pp. 445–463; cf. also Miranda, *Being and the Messiah*, pp. 188–189; Miguez-Bonino, *Doing Theology*, pp. 86–105.

28. Segundo, *The Liberation of Theology*, pp. 8–9.

29. Robert McAfee Brown, "A Preface and a Conclusion," in Sergio Torres and John Eagleson (eds.), *Theology in the Americas* (Orbis Books, 1976), p. xxvii, n. 9.

30. Conversation with Walter Harrelson, Pacific School of Religion, July 1977.

31. Rudolf Bultmann, *Theology of the New Testament*, tr. by Kendrick Grobel, Vol. I (Charles Scribner's Sons, 1951), p. 352.

32. Barth, *Church Dogmatics*, Vol. IV, Pt. 3, ii (1962), p. 558,

33. Conzelmann, *An Outline of the Theology of the New Testament,* p. 186.

34. *Ibid.,* pp. 256, 280.

35. Russell, *Ferment of Freedom,* Ch. 9, "A Future to Hope In," pp. 95–101.

GLOSSARY

ADVENTOLOGY A form of eschatology in which the future is interpreted as the *new* that is coming into history. It is concerned with the *Adventus* as God's future coming toward us in anticipation of the New Creation. (Ch. 8; see Eschatology.)

APOCALYPSE A form of eschatology present in the Bible in which the future is interpreted as *imminent* because the end of the age and the world is about to come to pass. (Ch. 8; see Eschatology.)

AXIOLOGY A form of eschatology in which the future is interpreted as taking place *now* in the center of personal history as we respond in faith to the hearing of the Word of God. (Ch. 8; see Eschatology.)

CHARISMATA The Greek word for "gifts" that signifies God's free gifts of the Spirit in the New Age. They are to be exercised through service in proportion to the gifts received. (Ch. 2.)

DIAKONIA The Greek word for "service," "ministry," or "servanthood," frequently used as a description of Jesus' own ministry and of the calling of Christians (Luke 4:18–19). (Ch. 3.)

ESCHATOLOGY Thinking *(logos)* about the end or goal of existence *(eschaton)*. Biblical eschatology is rooted in the hope of things to come which are not only future but also taking place in history now. There are various styles or forms of eschatology. (Ch. 8; see Adventology, Apocalypse, Axiology, Teleology.)

HERMENEUTICS The process of translation, explanation,

or interpretation of the Bible. The use of hermeneutics in the Bible is frequently eschatological. The writers look to God's promised future in order to interpret and understand the past and the present. (Ch. 8; see Eschatology.)

HETEROSEXISM A systemic form of oppression in which the beliefs and actions of society reinforce the "inherent superiority" of the heterosexual pattern of loving and thereby its right to dominance. Heterosexuals' fear and prejudice against homosexuals *(homophobia)* whose sexual orientation is toward those of the same sex. This "ism" is similar to *racism, sexism,* and *classism,* in which belief and action reinforce the "inherent superiority" of one group over the other. (Ch. 4.)

HOS ME The Greek words *hōs mē* are used by Paul meaning "as if not." Life in the New Creation is one that is lived now, in the midst of the world "as if (we did it) not" (I Cor. 7:29–31). Our actions and the way we order our lives and churches are of penultimate importance compared to the ultimate importance of the gift of God's love for humanity and the commission to proclaim the good news of that love. (Ch. 8.)

KLESIS The Greek word *klēsis* is usually translated "vocation" or "calling." It signifies God's call to freedom in a witnessing community. All Christians are called to live out the Christ event in their lives through service of God and neighbor. (Ch. 6.)

KOINONIA The word *koinōnia* in the Greek New Testament is translated "communion," "community," "participation," "partnership." Partnership for Christians can be described as a new focus of relationship in a common history of Jesus Christ that sets persons free for others. (Chs. 3, 8; see Partnership.)

NEW CREATION An eschatological concept used to designate the New Age of redemption. In Jesus Christ, God has decisively intervened in history and human life to establish the beginning of a New Age. We look to the fulfillment of the New Age or New Creation in which all creation will be set free. (Ch. 8; see Eschatology.)

OIKONOMIA The Greek word for "household management" or "stewardship," from the word *oikos,* meaning "house." God's *oikonomia* is God's plan or economy in the management of God's household (the world). Our *oikonomia* is partnership in God's saving activity in the world as stewards of New Creation. (Ch. 1.)

OPPRESSION A word used to designate systemic ways in which persons are denied their full humanity in society. Oppression has many forms—physical, psychological, social, political, economic, ecclesial. As distinguished from *deliberate oppression* through one's own actions, *systemic oppression* arises from the interaction of various elements comprising a social system. Thus racism, sexism, classism, and heterosexism exist without persons being consciously oppressive. (Ch. 6; see Heterosexism.)

PAROUSIA The Greek word in the New Testament meaning "coming." It is an eschatological word used in reference to the coming of the Messiah or Chosen One of God. (Ch. 8; see Eschatology.)

PARTNERSHIP A new focus of relationship in which there is continuing commitment and common struggle in interaction with a wider community context. Usually the gifts of *synergy* (total effect greater than the sum of the parts), *serendipity* (unexpected events), and *sharing* are present. (Ch. 8; see *Koinōnia.*)

TELEOLOGY A form of eschatology in which the future is interpreted as the *end* of life and the destiny of the soul. (Ch. 8; see Eschatology.)

TRADITION The dynamic and continuing process of God handing over Jesus Christ into the hands of all generations and nations is called *Tradition* or Traditioning (*paradosis,* Matt. 17:22; Rom. 8:31–33). The human process by which we choose from the still living and evolving past in order to shape the future is called *tradition.* Human customs and religious practices are called *traditions.* (Ch. 6.)

TRANSEUNT A form of the word "transient," which signifies "going beyond itself" and reflects the Latin trans*ire,* "to go beyond." Transeunce,the human ability to go beyond ourselves toward others in order to realize our own being, is often expressed through *diakonia,* or the service of others. (Ch. 2; see *Diakonia.*)

TRINITY The way we describe our experience of the mystery of God's saving action in and through Jesus Christ and the

Holy Spirit. The *economic Trinity* describes God's dynamic communication of love to the world, and the *immanent Trinity* describes God's dynamic self-communication of love between the persons of the Trinity. God has chosen to be partner with Godself and with us as Creator, Liberator, and Advocate. (Ch. 1; see *Oikonomia.*)

UTOPIA   Utopia literally means "no place" *(outopia)*. It can also mean "good place" *(eutopia)* in contrast to "bad place" *(dystopia)*. In the title of Chapter 2, utopia signifies a description of God's promised future and our place in that New Creation. (Ch. 3; see New Creation.)